Life in a new dimension

by DON DOUBLE

Whitaker House

PITTSBURGH and COLFAX STS., SPRINGDALE, PA 15144

LIFE IN A NEW DIMENSION

Don Double
32a Fore Street, St. Austell
Cornwall, PL25 5EP
England

© Copyright 1978 by Don Double
Printed in the United States of America
ISBN: 0-88368-083-1

All Bible quotations are from the King James Version of the Bible unless otherwise identified. Those identified *NASB* are from the *New American Standard Bible,* © The Lockman Foundation 1960, 1962, 1963, 1968, 1971, 1973, 1975, and are used by permission.

CONTENTS

FOREWORD

It is hardly possible to overestimate the power, love, joy and strength of character that can be ours through the simple truths revealed in this book. LIFE IN A NEW DIMENSION reminds us that when we became children of God, we acquired certain rights and privileges that are now our tremendous inheritance.

Through the years, I have experienced the blessings and principles Don Double shares here, and, as God is no respecter of persons, I can happily tell you that these blessings are available to you, too.

Don Gossett, author of
WHAT YOU SAY IS WHAT YOU GET!

NEW DIMENSION LIVING

I'm sure all of us as Christians have at some time prayed or desired to be like the Lord Jesus Christ. There is nothing higher to which we could attain than to be like Him, and this should be the goal of our Christian lives.

I believe this is what Paul had in mind when he wrote, "I press toward the mark for the prize of the high calling of God in Christ Jesus" (Philippians 3:14).

Paul knew he had not yet arrived at the place where he was like his Lord. But he was on the way. And I trust all who read this book are on the way, and that each will have that strong desire to become increasingly like Jesus Christ.

This likeness to Jesus, of course, is produced in our lives only by the working of the Holy Spirit. As we yield ourselves to Him, so He brings forth the fruit of the Spirit—love, joy, peace, patience, kindness, goodness, faithfulness, gentleness, self-control—which is in fact the character of Jesus.

But another requirement for likeness to the Lord

Jesus which is often overlooked, is that the gifts of the Spirit should also be flowing through our lives and ministries, just as they were through His.

If we agree that the fruit of the Spirit is the character of Jesus, let us also acknowledge that the gifts of the Spirit were the manifestation of the power in His earthly ministry. And if we really want to be like Him, then both are essential for us also.

Paul, writing to the Corinthian church, said, "Now concerning spiritual gifts, brethren, I would not have you ignorant" (1 Corinthians 12:1). God does not want us to be ignorant concerning His gifts. Yet, sadly, we do find much ignorance in this matter.

If you want a successful Christian life, I strongly recommend that you search out all the things concerning which the Bible says we should not be ignorant. And if you are a minister of the Word, I suggest you teach them very diligently to your flock. Hosea tells us that God's people "are destroyed for lack of knowledge" (Hosea 4:6).

In 1 Corinthians 12:1 and 2, Paul says clearly that Christians should not be ignorant of the gifts of the Spirit. He reminds the Corinthians of their former ignorance when as Gentiles they were "carried away unto these dumb idols." Christians should not be ignorant! There is no need. Neither should they be themselves like dumb idols! The gifts of the Spirit should be flowing through them.

Now I believe there are more than nine gifts of the Holy Spirit. In the Bible you will find other manifestations of the Spirit besides those listed in 1 Corinthians 12: 8-10. But for these studies, we will confine ourselves to the nine supernatural gifts mentioned here, before going on to take a closer look at the nine manifestations of the fruit of the Spirit recorded in Galatians 5:22 and 23.

And with each step may we discover the fullness of Life in an exciting new dimension.

Part One

OBTAINING POWER

CHAPTER 1

OPERATING BY LOVE

A crowd milled around the spacious home; friends, relatives, acquaintances, dressed in somber clothes of mourning. Many were in despair over the death of the man of the household, yet they had come in hopes of consoling the grieving family.

The sloping hills around the house were quiet, as though reflecting the loss of the mourners. Then someone spotted another mourner walking across the hills approaching the village; it was a late arrival who had been expected many days before. One member of the family rushed out to meet this friend, so glad that he had arrived and yet wondering why he hadn't come many days earlier. Soon after, the dead man's sister, hearing of the arrival of this friend, also ran quickly to meet him. But this time many of the mourners were following curiously.

In tears, the late arrival asked to be taken to the grave sight. As they all climbed the hill to the stone covered grave, many remarked at the love this friend had for the deceased man. Suddenly, the newcomer asked the family to have the large stone removed from the entrance of the tomb. A murmur went through the crowd. The family tried to quietly remind their friend that after four days the body would certainly smell. Undaunted, the man insisted that the stone be moved. After a short prayer, he turned toward the opening of the tomb and shouted,

"Lazarus, come forth!"

The crowd was stilled in amazement. Before their marveling eyes they saw a man, still wrapped in grave clothes, emerge slowly from the tomb. While they stood looking on in wonder, the powerful friend commanded, "Remove his wrappings and set him free."

Imagine the joy of the family who had loved this man, Lazarus. For he who was dead had risen to life, to lead their house again, to eat at their table, to share their joys and sorrows. No greater love could have been shown to them by their friend, Jesus Christ, at that moment, than to raise Lazarus from the dead. It was a manifestation of the Holy Spirit, operating by love.

The power of Jesus' earthly ministry to do these and other supernatural acts for those in need was promised to His believers before Jesus ascended into heaven. Jesus not only stated that His disciples would do the works that He did and greater ones (John 14:12), but He also promised that He would send the vital source that would give them this supernatural power (Acts 1:8). That source is the Holy Spirit.

It is necessary to remember that the Holy Spirit is a Person. He is not an "it." When we are baptized in the Holy Spirit, we have the *fullness* of the Person of the Holy Spirit within us. And I believe it is important to

12

see that the gifts of the Spirit—which are the power of God in our lives—are resident in the Holy Spirit—in us. We should not be looking for the gifts of the Spirit to come from outside of ourselves, because they are in the Holy Spirit—in me—in you. You can never possess a gift of the Holy Spirit. The gift always belongs to the Holy Spirit—in you.

The nine gifts of the Spirit that we will cover here are listed in 1 Corinthians 12:8-10: "For to one is given by the Spirit the word of wisdom; to another the word of knowledge by the same Spirit; to another faith by the same Spirit; to another the gifts of healing by the same Spirit; to another the working of miracles; to another prophecy; to another discerning of spirits; to another divers kinds of tongues; to another the interpretation of tongues. . . ."

Paul then goes on to tell us that the Holy Spirit is in total charge of these gifts, "distributing to each one individually just as He wills" (1 Corinthians 12:11 *NASB*).

So for the gifts of the Spirit to operate through us, there must be total submission of us and *our* will to the Holy Spirit and *His* will. When we go to a meeting, we should prepare our hearts by consciously submitting to the Holy Spirit, saying in our hearts, "I am ready to be used, Lord Jesus, by the power of the Holy Spirit, the moment You want to use me."

First Corinthians 12:31 also urges us to "covet earnestly the best gifts." In the realm of spiritual gifts, we should be a covetous people. And we should not covet lightly. We should put our whole selves into the business of coveting earnestly the best gifts.

One other thing to keep in mind as we cover each of

13

these gifts in the following chapters, is that often one of the gifts of the Spirit is manifested in conjunction with another. For example, the gift of knowledge might come through a prophecy, or the gift of faith might accompany the working of miracles.

But before we go any further, we need to settle the question: Which are the best gifts? When many Christians are asked their opinion as to the best gift, they will answer "Love." But I am afraid I disagree with that, because love is not a gift. It is a fruit of the Spirit (Galatians 5:22).

The best gift, I believe, is the one needed at any given moment. We should be so submitted to the Holy Spirit that when a gift is needed He can use us in that particular gift required at the time.

And, when Paul goes on to say, "Yet show I unto you a more excellent way" (1 Corinthians 12:31), I believe he wants us to understand that the more excellent way is to have the gifts of the Spirit operating by the love of God.

If you owned a beautiful, new car with a smooth working engine, would you leave it sitting in your garage? And if you wanted to take your family out somewhere, would you expect to push the car out of the garage and down the highways to reach your destination?

That is what the Christian walk is like when we attempt to move in the love of God without the accompanying power of the Holy Spirit. The car can be likened to our salvation and the engine to the love which is so essential for our Christian walk. But for that car to work effectively, as it was created, it needs gasoline in the engine to give it power! The gifts of the Spirit are like that gasoline; they give us the power and ability to move effectively in the Kingdom of God, using our engine of love to its fullest.

To say "Well, I'll just have the love of God, and you can have the gifts" is like having the car and the engine but no gasoline! It finds us unable to do nearly as much to meet the needs of our generation. It finds us unable to do the loving act as Jesus did in any given situation, healing the sick, raising the dead, casting demons out of the possessed, comforting the discouraged with supernatural wisdom or prophecy.

Furthermore, 1 Corinthians 12:7 tells us that "to each one is given the manifestation of the Spirit for the common good" (*NASB*). I believe that every Spirit-filled believer should be used in the gifts of the Spirit that we might all lovingly benefit the entire Body of Christ.

In the average assembly today, you can generally find just one or two people (if any) exercising the gifts. I believe it is God's will that all should do so. I trust the Holy Spirit will firmly plant within your heart the vision of the whole Body of Christ functioning together.

Ephesians 4:16 speaks of "the whole body, being fitted and held together by that which every joint supplies" (*NASB*). Many of our problems come from lack of supply due to the fact that many of the joints in the Body of Christ have become stiff and are not working. The same verse goes on to tell us that we all grow up in love whenever the gifts are operating; "... according to the proper working of each individual part, causes the growth of the body for the building up of itself in love."

I find it very exciting to be in meetings where the gifts

of the Spirit are operating. It decentralizes the meeting from around one man. You never know what is going to happen next. When a company of the Lord's people come together, I believe it is God's will that He be given the opportunity to meet the needs of everyone present. He cannot do that through one man. But He can do it through the Body of Christ as the gifts of the Spirit operate.

Finally, in case you think you have to be a really mature Christian before exercising the gifts of the Spirit, I know a man who was saved, baptized in the Spirit, and used in the gift of prophecy, all within twenty minutes! So if you've been saved longer than twenty minutes, it's time you too were moving out into the realm of the gifts of the Spirit.

CHAPTER 2

THE WORD OF WISDOM

"For to one is given by the Spirit the word of wisdom..."

Let us recognize, first of all, that the nine gifts of the Holy Spirit are supernatural. These are not human gifts. There is nothing natural about them. The word of wisdom is not a wisdom that can be learned. It is supernaturally imparted by God, the Holy Spirit—a fragment of *His* wisdom. And it is supernaturally communicated for a given purpose.

There is an excellent example of the word of wisdom in the ministry of the Lord Jesus, in John's Gospel, chapter eight. The Pharisees caught a woman in the very act of adultery and brought her to Jesus with the challenge, "Moses in the law commanded us, that such should be stoned: but what sayest thou?" They were trying to trap Jesus into saying something for which they could accuse and criticize Him. Jesus simply replied, "He that is without sin among you, let him first cast a stone at her," and went on writing on the ground.

When He looked up, all those who had accused the woman were gone.

In such a situation, the natural human thing to do would be to argue—to engage in wordy discussion. How many hours have we wasted on discussion in the Lord's work, when all we really needed was a supernatural word of wisdom?

The Lord Jesus didn't bother to parley with the Pharisees. The word of wisdom went beyond all argument and pierced their hearts, dispersing the accusers. It was all over in a short time.

On another occasion, Jesus used the word of wisdom when dealing with the conniving Pharisees. Wanting to trick Jesus into either defending or maligning Caesar, they asked Him, "Is it lawful to give tribute unto Caesar, or not?" But Jesus perceived their malice and asked them to show Him the coin used for the tax. Holding up the coin, He asked whose image and inscription were on the money. When they answered, "Caesar's," Jesus wisely replied, "Render therefore unto Caesar the things which are Caesar's, and unto God the things that are God's." And "When they heard these words, they marveled..." (Matthew 22:17-21).

That is what a supernatural word of wisdom will do for us, it will cause people to marvel at the greatness of Jesus Christ in us.

We find the word of wisdom in the Old Testament, too. First Kings 3:16-28 gives the story of two harlots who came to Solomon. Each had born a child about the same time. During the night one baby died, and the mother of the dead child exchanged it for the living one, while the other mother slept. Now they came to Solomon for judgment, each claiming the living child as her own.

What a predicament! In the natural, Solomon had no way of discerning the truth. But God gave him a word of wisdom. Solomon said, "Bring me a sword: I will cut this baby in half, and give half to each." Immediately, the mother of the living child cried out, "No, don't do that!" Whereas the one who was not the mother maliciously agreed it should be done.

In this way, Solomon knew the identity of the true mother, and gave her the baby. Solomon received the solution to the problem by the wisdom of God. Verse 28 of the same passage says, "... they saw that the wisdom of God was in him." This is exactly what the word of wisdom is: the wisdom of God supernaturally imparted within us.

I believe that there are many times when we need the wisdom of God. I remember one occasion in my ministry, when a person who had an evil spirit came to me for prayer. As I was about to pray, the Lord said, *"Ask him if he is born again."* The man replied that he was not. I asked him if after God delivered him, he would give his life to Christ, and he answered, "No, I am not prepared to do that." So I replied, "Then I am sorry, I cannot pray for you. According to Matthew 12:43-45, if I cast that evil spirit out of you, I will be exposing you to a worse condition. The evil spirit would find seven other spirits, bring them back into you, and your last state would be worse than the first."

There are times and situations like this when we desperately need the wisdom of God. Through the authority the Lord Jesus has given us, those evil spirits have to do what we tell them in Jesus' name. They have no choice. But if people are not willing to yield to the

Lord, the evil spirits only go out the front door and in again at the back, bringing others with them.

We often need the word of wisdom to operate the other gifts, lest we go rushing in like fools "where angels fear to tread."

The word of wisdom is also very vital in church discipline and government. In Acts 6:1-7, we find the apostles receiving a word of wisdom concerning the problems of serving tables and the widows who were being neglected. The Bible tells us that the twelve apostles wisely responded to this situation by saying, "It is not desirable for us to neglect the word of God in order to serve tables. But select from among you, brethren, seven men of good reputation, full of the spirit and of wisdom, whom we may put in charge of this task" (*NASB*). This was certainly a word of wisdom, for it not only took care of the situation, but the Bible goes on to say that the decision "found approval with the whole congregation."

The word of wisdom can be a great blessing to the local church and keep boards of elders and entire congregations from disagreements over the word of God.

On one occasion, God gave a word of wisdom in a potentially difficult situation, and saved our Good News Crusade team from a lot of trouble.

A ten-year-old boy had received Jesus at one of our pre-crusade rallies led by my son-in-law, Simon Matthews.

This lad happened to be a choirboy in a local church. When his choir master saw his decision card, he was angry that the boy had believed he was a sinner in need of a Savior. He contacted the boy's mother and began to stir up a storm.

The story got into the local paper and actually gave us some free publicity. Several extra people supported the crusade as a direct result. But that was not the end.

A reporter from a national Sunday newspaper, looking for a good smear story, began to chase me around the country by telephone. He eventually caught up with me, and began to fire his questions.

"Now, what exactly are you saying happened to this boy?" he pounced eagerly.

At that point, the Lord gave me what I believe was a word of wisdom, and I replied calmly, "The same thing that happened to Dr. David Livingstone (the famous Scottish missionary) at approximately the same age."

For some reason, this answer absolutely floored the reporter, and he more or less dropped that aspect of the subject. Instead, he grilled me for about twenty minutes concerning the Good News Crusade, trying to get another angle on us, but without success. Finally, nothing appeared in the national press concerning my interview with him at all. The word of wisdom had saved us from a tricky situation.

A further example of a very simple, but effective, word of wisdom comes from a missionary friend of mine in Japan.

A tent campaign had been planned for a certain small, strongly Buddhist town, where there was no church or Christian witness. The sponsoring pastor (from a church in a nearby town), together with my missionary friend, went to the town office to ask permission to use a certain site to pitch the tent.

Other times when this pastor had made requests, such as for the hiring of a hall to hold meetings, he had always been refused.

Entering the office, the two men found, to their dismay, that they faced the same official who consistently turned the pastor down. As anticipated, he greeted them expressionlessly and acted in his usual negative fashion. However, to reinforce his refusal, he went and checked with one of his peers.

After a few moments he returned and confirmed with obvious satisfaction, "No, it is out of the question. We are going to build houses on that land."

Meanwhile, the missionary, not prepared to take Satan's refusal as an answer, had been praying softly in tongues. He now entered the conversation and found himself saying, "You mean you are going to build houses on *all* that land?"

"Ah-er, we-er, B-b-b," the official began to splutter (in Japanese of course!). In complete confusion, he withdrew to ask someone else's opinion, saving his own face in the bargain.

Eventually, he returned and announced sheepishly that permission had been granted to use the site. For some reason, known only to God, those words had been just the right ones to turn the situation around.

How we all need wisdom at times like these, for some simple appropriate word will often turn the tables on the opposition and put the enemy to flight.

I want to be constantly in the place where God can supernaturally impart His wisdom to me whenever I need it. Don't you?

CHAPTER 3

THE WORD OF KNOWLEDGE

Its Uses

". . . to another the word of knowledge by the same Spirit"

Just as the word of wisdom is a fragment of God's wisdom, so the word of knowledge is a fragment of God's knowledge—also supernaturally given.

In considering the word of knowledge, it is good to remind ourselves that God knows everything. He is "Alpha and Omega," the beginning and the end. He knows every single thing there is to know. He not only knows *what* we do, but *why* we do it.

In the Christian life, motives count more than actions. An action can look right and scriptural, but the motive can be very wrong. The word of knowledge often operates in personal counseling, revealing motives and showing a person why things have gone wrong.

As far as I can tell, the word of knowledge is the most recorded gift in the Bible. Yet it is so little taught in the church today. We hear much about the gift of tongues.

Many books have been written on the subject. There are also several books on the gift of prophecy, and not a few on the healing ministry. But I personally only know of one book written on the word of knowledge. General teaching on the gifts usually passes over it very quickly. Yet if the Bible takes the trouble to record it more than any other gift, the word of knowledge is surely very important.

Let us look at an instance in Scripture where this gift was used. First Kings 14:1-6:

"At that time Abijah the son of Jeroboam fell sick. And Jeroboam said to his wife, Arise, I pray thee, and disguise thyself, that thou be not known to be the wife of Jeroboam; and get thee to Shiloh: behold, there is Ahijah the prophet, which told me that I should be king over this people.... He shall tell thee what shall become of the child" (verses 1-3).

Jeroboam wanted his wife to be deceitful, not because there was anything wrong with the question she was going to ask, but because he knew he was out of favor with the prophet and with God.

In verse four we notice that "Ahijah could not see; for his eyes were set by reason of his age." In other words, he was blind. In verses five and six the word of knowledge comes into operation:

"And the Lord said unto Ahijah, Behold, the wife of Jeroboam cometh to ask a thing of thee for her son; for he is sick: thus and thus shalt thou say unto her: for it shall be, when she cometh in, that she shall feign herself to be another woman. And it was so, when Ahijah heard the sound of her feet, as she came in at the door, that he said, Come in, thou wife of Jeroboam; why feignest thou thyself to be another? for I am sent to thee with heavy tidings" (verses 5-6).

What a shock it must have been to her! She had gone to all the trouble to disguise herself. I'm sure she had rehearsed many times so that her voice would sound different! But she didn't even get the chance to use her voice. God was one step ahead. "Come in, thou wife of Jeroboam."

We need to realize that the word of knowledge is very valuable in our churches to keep them clean from deceitfulness. And we ought to recognize that God could use the gift to keep each of us clean, too. If the word of knowledge was in operation more, I believe we'd know more of the power of God in our churches, for they would be sanctified churches.

This gift was often in operation in the ministry of the Lord Jesus. When the woman of Samaria (John 4) met the Lord at Jacob's well, He began to talk to her about living water. At last she came to the place where she said, "Give me this water." When Jesus replied, "Go, call your husband," the woman answered, "I don't have one." And then Jesus said something like this, "That's right, you don't have one; you've had five, and the one you have now is not yours."

I see something very important in the exercise of the word of knowledge here. I believe the Church is full of problems today because of the lack of the use of the word of knowledge. There has been a type of evangelism that says, "Come to Jesus. Only believe!" But that is not what the Bible teaches. The Bible says, "Repent and believe." If there is no call for repentance, you end up with what we call "believism," which produces a type of Christian constantly living in problems.

25

It was Wesley who said, "Repentance unlocks the door to the new birth." If, right at the beginning, we were supernaturally minded for the gifts of the Spirit, the Lord would use the gifts through us to produce a thorough work of repentance in the people.

Right at the beginning of their Christian lives they would be cleaned up, and the work of grace would go tremendously deep, saving hours and hours of counseling afterwards. Remember the Lord Jesus said on another occasion, "Unless you repent...you perish."

This is what the Lord was after in His dealings with the woman of Samaria. He used the word of knowledge, coming right to the root of her problem, to produce a true repentance.

I remember a friend of mine, a tremendous man of God, sharing an experience with me. He has the most amazing exercise of the gift of knowledge I have ever known. One night he was ministering the word and many people needed counseling. There wasn't time to see them all that evening, so it was arranged for them to meet him at half-hourly intervals throughout the next morning.

One woman had an appointment for eleven o'clock. She walked in at twenty-five minutes past eleven; the next person's appointment was set for eleven-thirty. As this young lady entered, my friend received a word of knowledge. He said, "Sit down." He didn't bother to ask why she had come. He simply continued, "You are a prostitute. The reason you are late is that you have just been with a man." With that she dropped on her knees crying out for mercy, and was gloriously delivered by the grace of God. A word of knowledge saves a tremendous amount of time!

I believe, as ministers of God, our time is very precious. We waste many hours trying to probe around with people when, if we would believe God, there is supernatural knowledge available that could take us straight to the point. It would bring tremendous respect to the church.

In Acts, chapter 5, we see the word of knowledge in operation in the early church. Ananias and Sapphira had sold their piece of land. Everybody else had voluntarily given all they possessed. Ananias and Sapphira decided they would like to keep a little for themselves; and there was nothing wrong with that. The Bible tells us to give as we have purposed in our hearts. But, they wanted to look like the rest. So Ananias presented his money at the apostles' feet, as if he was giving it all.

In Acts 5:3-4 Peter exercises the word of knowledge, "Ananias, why has Satan filled your heart to lie to the Holy Spirit, and to keep back some of the price of the land? While it remained unsold, did it not remain your own? And after it was sold, was it not under your control? Why is it that you have conceived this deed in your heart? You have not lied to men, but to God" (*NASB*).

Ananias, hearing this, fell down and died. The same thing happened to Sapphira. This is supernatural discipline by the word of knowledge. And I believe God is restoring this to the church.

I like what it says in verse 11: "And great fear came upon all the church, and upon as many as heard these things." I pray that great fear will come upon the church in these days in which we live—the righteous fear of the Lord.

I honestly don't believe it's possible to have the fear of the Lord without a manifestation of the supernatural. Without the supernatural element, we just live as natural people in a natural consciousness that has no fear of God in it.

In a conference recently, God gave a word of knowledge to the effect that a certain businessman present in the meeting had become unwillingly involved in a transaction which had become deceitful, and couldn't find a way out. He was now living under condemnation. God sent this word of knowledge, that if the man would respond, He would show him the answer. Isn't the Lord good? That shows me how much God loves us.

Many times, because of the lack of the manifestation of the supernatural, people have gone on for years under condemnation. That is cruel. God doesn't want a church walking around under the weight of condemnation. "There is therefore now no condemnation to them which are in Christ Jesus..." (Romans 8:1). And I believe one of the manifestations of the word of knowledge is to keep the church free from condemnation.

Another time there was a farmer in the meeting who was about to go bankrupt. We didn't know the man, but God revealed these facts through the word of knowledge. If he would come and make himself known, God would give him the solution. It was a very simple one! The Lord told him he hadn't been paying his tithes. The Bible says that if we pay our tithes the Lord will "rebuke the devourer" for our sakes. The Lord said He would forgive the farmer if he started paying his tithes then. Yes, the Lord is even interested in our business lives.

Also, this gift operates to produce faith in people's hearts for healing. God reveals that there are people with certain physical conditions in the meeting. As He reveals this, it is like a word of faith to them. They respond and He heals them.

I remember when I was in East Africa, lying on the bed one day preparing for the evening service, when God showed me someone would be healed that night of a serious pain in the back.

I walked to the meeting that evening with a married woman missionary who was a nurse. I had never used the gift of the word of knowledge before in East Africa, and as I was to be interpreted into Swahili, I told her what God had said and asked if it would translate correctly.

She looked me right in the eyes and said, "Don, do you think it could be me?" She explained that when her first child was born she injured her back and had been in constant pain ever since. Any time she had extra work the pain became very severe, and pain-killers didn't help. So right there, on the way to the church, we stopped and prayed for her, and the Lord healed her back instantly, making her every whit whole.

How wonderful when God gives a word of knowledge in this way!

CHAPTER 4

THE WORD OF KNOWLEDGE

How It Operates

How does the gift of the word of knowledge operate? Most commonly the knowledge just comes. If you have ever been used in the gift of prophecy you will understand, as it comes in a very similar way.

It is very important of course that we are "in faith." It's profitable to learn this basic lesson, because it operates in all realms of our relationship with God. In ministry, God can only speak to faith. If you are in unbelief, it's obvious God cannot speak to you, because you will doubt whether or not it is God speaking.

A person will wonder, "Is it me, is it the Lord?" "Is it the Lord, is it my mind?" Another queries, "Is it the Lord, is it the devil?" Unbelief will always cause confusion. We must come to the place of faith. When you have arrived there, you believe everything that comes to you is from God.

Before I go to a meeting, I always prepare my heart by doing certain things. First of all, I ask God for a fresh cleansing in the precious blood of Jesus. Then I am sanctified in spirit, soul and body. At that point, I am perfectly clean and can come boldly before the throne of grace.

I also ask the Lord to give me a fresh filling or anointing of the Holy Spirit. I then make a deliberate commitment of myself to the realm of the Holy Spirit. Finally, I take the authority God has given me and bind every power of the devil. I then go to the meeting with faith in that which I have prayed, and I believe that only God can speak to me. Everything that comes I take by faith to be from the Lord.

If by chance (and I say if) I slip somewhere and fall from faith, I know immediately. There's no problem about knowing—my peace is disturbed. The Bible tells us, "Let the peace of God rule (umpire, give the final decision) in your hearts" (Colossians 3:15). So, I am in a perfect place of safety.

I believe God loves us so much that He wants us to be in the Spirit, in the place of faith, and used in the gifts, even more than we do. So there are no problems from God's side. And if I want to be in the Spirit, in the place of faith, and desire God to use me more than anything else, there are no problems from my side. If I'm willing to believe that, then there is nothing to stop me—as long as I'm prepared to step out in faith.

A second way the word of knowledge seems to operate is what we call "seeing in our spirit." The Bible uses the term "perceiving in our spirit" (see Mark 2:8). In Acts 14:9-10 we read concerning a certain cripple, "The same heard Paul speak: who steadfastly beholding him, and perceiving that he had faith to be healed, said with a loud voice, Stand upright on thy feet...." Paul perceived in his spirit. He saw that the man had faith to be healed.

You can see many things in your spirit. In fact, as far as the spiritual realm is concerned, it is more important to see in your spirit than to see with your natural eyes.

For example, you may be standing in front of someone to pray for them to be healed. And God will show you the form of a person, and you see a little black spot on his chest. That indicates there is something wrong with his lungs.

I remember on one occasion seeing in my spirit a picture of a leg with a chain around it. It was chained to the wall and kept pulling, trying to get away. The moment I described what I was seeing, a woman doctor in the meeting cried, "It's me! It's me!" She had been a member of an exclusive group for many years, and although baptized in the Holy Spirit, still could not break free. That morning we prayed for her and God snapped the chains.

There is another way the word of knowledge operates as far as sick people are concerned. You may be in a meeting when suddenly you feel a pain in your body somewhere. It's not because you are sick. God is showing you there is someone in the meeting with a pain like that whom He wants to heal. For instance, you feel a pain in your knee. You simply say, "There is someone here with a pain in the knee whom God wants to heal." The person responds, you pray for them, and they are healed!

In one of our tent meetings, God showed me someone had stomach trouble. This person had tried medical science, but the doctors could not discover what was wrong. When I announced this, I was amazed to see the local doctor come forward. He told me he'd been to the hospital and had internal examinations, but they could not diagnose his complaint. We prayed for him, and the Lord instantly healed him. His written testimony is still on my files.

We read of the Lord Jesus that He can be "touched with the feeling of our infirmities." If He can be touched with the feeling of our infirmities, then it is very simple for Him to impart what He feels into our bodies so that we feel it. But don't accept it as a sickness for yourself! It's not for you, but a signal for you to minister out to others.

One final word. There is a need to beware of counterfeit gifts. I do not say this to produce a wrong kind of fear. Remember that for every counterfeit there has to be a genuine article. But the devil is ever busy counterfeiting what God is doing. The Bible says that "Satan himself is transformed into an angel of light." Satan always comes as near to the truth as he can in order to deceive, and yet there will be a flaw somewhere.

There is an occult fad which is very popular today called ESP (extrasensory perception). One of the things about ESP is that it is often accurate, and many people are deceived for that reason. I am not impressed by someone who can supernaturally reveal things correctly.

In Acts 16 the girl who had a spirit of divination was accurate when she said, "These men are the servants of the Most High God. . . ." But Paul and Silas didn't turn around to her and say "Hallelujah!" They turned and said to the spirit, "I command thee in the name of Jesus Christ to come out of her." In spite of the girl being accurate, she needed deliverance by the power of God.

In John 1:47-49 an important principle emerges. "Jesus saw Nathanael coming to Him, and said of him,

'Behold, an Israelite indeed, in whom is no guile!' Nathanael said to Him, 'How do you know me?' Jesus answered and said to him, 'Before Phillip called you, when you were under the fig tree, I saw you.' Nathanael answered Him, 'Rabbi, You are the Son of God; You are the King of Israel'"(*NASB*).

The Lord used the word of knowledge and told Nathanael He saw him under the fig tree before Phillip called him. Nathanael's immediate response was, "Rabbi, You are the Son of God; You are the King of Israel." In other words, the word of knowledge centralized itself in the Lord Jesus and glorified Him.

I always like to feel at the end of a meeting that the people are talking about Jesus as they go home. If they are talking about Don Double, I feel very concerned.

Beware of anything that glorifies the one being used and makes the channel look like some great person. The Bible is quite clear that the ministry of the Holy Spirit is to glorify Jesus Christ.

If you see supernatural gifts operating and feel like saying, "Praise the Lord! Wonderful Jesus!" then you know that all is well. But if you feel, "My, that minister's tremendous! That person's great! What a wonderful gift!" then be on your guard.

The true gifts of the Holy Spirit will always centralize themselves in the Lord Jesus Christ, and glorify *Him*.

CHAPTER 5

THE GIFT OF FAITH

"... to another faith by the same Spirit"

There are three realms of faith. The first you will find in Romans 12:3, "... God hath dealt to every man the measure of faith." God has given each of us the ability to believe Him. I call this natural faith. If someone says to me, "I don't have any faith," I tell him he must know more than God because God says he does have faith. This faith is never the gift of faith because it is a natural faith.

In 2 Thessalonians 1:3 Paul tells the Christians, "your faith groweth exceedingly." Notice it is "their" faith, and their faith is growing. As we feed upon the Word of God, our natural faith does grow.

Some people's faith grows so exceedingly that when you're around them you just feel their faith rubbing off on yourself. I like being with that kind of person. He's always talking positively, always talking about what the Lord can do, always believing Him for great things, always living in God's supply. But it's still the natural faith that has grown and matured into something tremendous. I trust your natural faith is growing. And although it is the natural faith common to us all, I don't want to belittle it. It is very important.

The second realm of faith is in Galatians 5:22. This faith is the fruit of faith which I look upon as faithfulness. But we will be dealing with this aspect of faith in the second section of the book under the fruit of the Spirit.

The third realm of faith is of course the gift of faith which is the main subject of our chapter.

I believe the gift of faith is to be supernaturally emptied of all doubt. And no one is like that all the time. Like the other gifts of the Spirit, it is supernaturally imparted for a given occasion. If we had the gift of faith all the time, we could empty the hospitals and do away with every problem. But God in His wisdom does not give it to us all the time.

If we are honest, every one of us will admit that although we have natural faith and the fruit of faith, there are times when doubts and unbelief assail us. But when the gift of faith operates, it is impossible to doubt, because you are supernaturally emptied of all doubt.

After Jesus cursed the fig tree (Mark 11), Peter said to Him in amazement, "Behold, the fig tree which you cursed has withered." It was as if Peter were asking, "How did You do that, Lord?" And Jesus replied, "Have the faith of God." He was really saying, "I did it by God's faith." And that is exactly what the gift of faith is—God's faith.

It is the faith that spoke this universe into existence. Sorry, I don't believe in evolution; I believe God spoke this world into being. It exists today because of God's faith. And when the gift of faith operates, it is that kind of faith—tremendous.

I remember once when God allowed the gift to come upon me. I stood up in a meeting and said, *"I guarantee that every sick person here tonight who comes forward will be healed."* As I listened to myself say it, my natural mind was really surprised. There were all sorts of sick people there! But my spirit was so full of faith and assurance that the momentary surprise was quickly dispelled.

As the people came hobbling out on sticks and crutches (and it wasn't hard to get people up to be prayed for that night), God healed every single one of them! They threw away their sticks and crutches and were absolutely whole. I wish that would happen every night. But it doesn't, because it is "just as *He* wills."

On another occasion, we were conducting a meeting on a cold, snowy night. This particular evening, my brother-in-law asked if he could put his dog in my van during the meeting. After the meeting, I had numerous people to counsel and pray with, so my brother-in-law asked for the keys to get his dog out, saying he would leave them in the van afterwards.

He took the keys and unlocked the door. After taking the dog out, he inadvertently shut and locked the door with the keys remaining in the ignition.

Eventually, very late at night, my team and I went to the van. I went to open the door but found I couldn't. It was bitterly cold, and everyone in the village seemed to have gone to bed. Among the team was a young lady who had a small baby at home needing to be fed. With her home being eight or nine miles away, she was the most concerned of all of us about getting home and suggested we have some prayer.

As we were praying, the Holy Spirit spoke very clearly saying, *"Go and open the door."* At that moment, I was supernaturally emptied of all doubt. God filled me with such faith, I knew I would be able to open the door with no problems. So, as the rest were praying, I walked to the van and pulled on the door. And, the locked door simply opened without the need of a key or any device to unlock it. Hallelujah!

God had given me a special gift of faith to know that the door would open when I pulled on it. After the door opened, this gift of faith left me. I do not have the faith to open every locked door I come to, but with the supernatural gift of faith, it was possible in that specific instance. It was a tremendous experience! To this day, it has continued to encourage me and those that were with me that night.

Some scripture references showing the gift of faith in operation can be found in the ministry of Elijah.

In I Kings 18:20-40 we have the story of Elijah calling down fire from heaven. Elijah had challenged the prophets of Baal to build an altar and to place an ox on it, calling on their god to send down fire from heaven to consume the sacrifice. Elijah was going to set up a similar altar, calling on the one true God to do the same. Elijah was so full of faith that he mocked the prophets of Baal for their vain efforts before he had even attempted the feat! What's more, he had three buckets of water thrown on his altar so that the Lord Jehovah would have to do a very mighty miracle. And of course He did, as fire rained down from heaven and consumed the ox, the altar *and* the water! As the gift of faith was operating for Elijah, no doubts could trouble him.

Finally, the gift of faith is also seen in operation in the story of the centurion whose servant was dying, recorded in Matthew 8:5-13. When the centurion approached Jesus, the Lord offered to come to his house and heal the slave. But the centurion answered the Lord in words of powerful faith, "Lord, I am not worthy that thou shouldst come under my roof: but speak the word only, and my servant shall be healed."

The centurion was so full of faith that he didn't even need to have the Lord touch his servant or enter his house. And "When Jesus heard it, he marveled, and said to them that followed. . . . I have not found so great faith, no, not in Israel." By the time the centurion returned to his home, the servant was healed!

There wasn't a doubt in this centurion's mind— because he was exercising the gift of faith.

CHAPTER 6

GIFTS OF HEALING

"...to another the gifts of healing by the same Spirit"

I believe that the reason that this gift is described in the plural is that God gives different gifts of healing to various members of the Body of Christ, at different times, to reach different areas of sickness. When the gifts of healing are operating, some ministries have a high rate of success with certain types of diseases, and very moderate results with others.

I have found in my own ministry, at times, a high rate of success with arthritic cases. At some periods, I have had tremendous success with blind people. At other times with the deaf. The only explanation that I can give is that a gift of healing was operating in that particular area.

Now I don't believe that anyone should be able to say that they have the gifts of healing operating in their lives at all times. I believe the gifts of healing, like the other gifts, are a supernatural impartation for a given occasion, and that no one constantly has these gifts operating in his ministry. Sometimes when we pray for the sick, it is obvious that the gifts of healing are operating. At other times, it is as equally evident that they are not, and we are just down to praying for the sick in obedience to the Word, with our ordinary faith.

There was one evangelist from South Africa that began to walk in the power of the gifts of healing early in his ministry. It began when the Holy Spirit blessed him with the gift of the healing of paralysis.

The first one to be healed was a young woman who was bedridden from a back injury at the factory where she worked. There was little hope for her recovery. But after this young evangelist prayed for her, she jumped out of bed and walked for the first time in nineteen months. She had been healed by the gift of healing operating through that man of God.

One night shortly after, there was a young ten-year-old boy who was carried into the evangelist's meeting on a stretcher and in a full body brace. He had an incurable disease of his joints and was paralyzed. But he believed in the power of Jesus to heal, so the evangelist unstrapped him from his bed. Immediately, the child began walking without help, his young face lit up with joy.

A final confirmation of the gift that was operating in the evangelist's life at the time was another young boy who was unable to walk. As he was prayed for, his mother unwrapped his bandages. Soon after, the young boy was dancing a jig in front of everyone, praising God for his healing. As a result, this boy's father was marvelously saved.

The gift of healing for these paralytic cases had

brought great joy and salvation to the lives it touched, just as in Jesus' day, and it confirmed to this man of God that the Holy Spirit would really bless him with the gifts of healing as he walked in faith.

It is also important to notice that when the gifts of healing are operating, it is not essential that the sick person himself has faith. I have seen in our crusades occasions when someone has told us he didn't believe God could heal him. Yet we prayed, and the Lord did heal. That was also a gift of healing.

Quite recently, I was preaching at a renewal rally in an Anglican Church in Tunbridge Wells, England. Among the congregation of about five or six hundred sat a woman who had been crippled with arthritis for many years.

As she listened to a sermon on the subject of healing, she reacted unfavorably, and decided that she disliked me very much. She didn't care for the conviction and assurance with which I presented the message.

In spite of this attitude, she came out for prayer, but became even more incensed as she heard me praying for one and another, and counseling, still with the same definiteness and assurance. Having suffered so long, she resented what must have sounded like an over-simplification of the problem. Any faith she had hit rock bottom.

Yet, as I prayed for this lady, she was instantly healed. She phoned in her testimony later, saying, "All pain left, and it has not returned. I am completely free from arthritis after many years of suffering."

That, I believe, was the working of a gift of healing.

In the Gospels when the Lord Jesus healed people, one of His most common observations was, "Thy faith hath saved thee" or, "Thy faith hath made thee whole." But there were other occasions in His ministry when it appears that the person healed had nothing to do with it, and faith is not mentioned.

Luke 14:4 is a case in point. It simply reads, "And he took him, and healed him, and let him go." That is a perfect example of a gift of healing operating. As I have said before, if we permanently had the gifts of healing resident in our lives and ministries, we could go and empty the hospitals. But as with all the other gifts, 1 Corinthians 12:11 is still relevant. The Holy Spirit gives these manifestations "to each one individually just as He wills."

CHAPTER 7

THE WORKING OF MIRACLES

"...to another the working of miracles"

I do not believe that the working of miracles is in any way confined to healing. It has a far wider scope than just the healing ministry. Of course, when parts of the body that were gone are re-created—that is a miracle.

In Japan, recently, we encountered a young man who had been without one eardrum since he was six years old. God gave him a new one and restored his hearing. That was a miracle.

There is also a certain Gospel singer with an international ministry who was born blind, without any pupils. But God is slowly restoring her pupils and they can even be seen growing back. Soon her entire sight will be restored. That is a miracle.

A good scriptural example of this distinction between a healing and a miracle is in Luke 17:19 in the story of the ten lepers. All were cleansed; their leprosy was healed. But the one who came back to thank Jesus was "made whole."

Leprosy eats away the extremities. I have personally seen lepers who have been healed medically. They are absolutely clean—no leprosy left on them. But their fingers and toes are stumps, and their ears have pieces missing. Yet there is no question that they are healed.

In the story of the ten lepers, only one was *made whole*. I believe that means that his fingers and toes grew again. That is the difference between being cleansed and being made whole. Nine of the lepers received healing, but one received "the working of miracles."

Another major example of miracles is the raising of the dead. Jesus showed this power in His own ministry with the raising of Lazarus (John, chapter eleven) and of Jarius' daughter (Luke, chapter eight).

Peter utilized this gift of miracles in Acts 9:36-42 when he was told that Tabitha (or Dorcas) a "woman abounding with deeds of goodness and charity" had fallen sick and died. Peter went quickly to her bedside where her mourning relatives and friends were weeping. The Bible says:

"Peter sent them all out and knelt down and prayed, and turning to her body he said, 'Tabitha, arise'" (*NASB*). And she did! When Peter presented her alive to her friends and loved ones, many people in the community came to believe in the Lord because of this miracle. The working of miracles should always draw people to Jesus Christ.

Paul also experienced the raising of the dead in Acts 20:7-12. A young disciple by the name of Eutychus fell asleep as Paul was preaching late at night and fell out of a three-story window! He was found dead on the ground below. But Paul quickly went down and embraced

Eutychus and gave him to his family, "and they took away the boy alive."

That was a miracle!

In Acts 8:6 we read that Philip was also used in the working of miracles.

Outside the ministry of healing, a tremendous example of the working of miracles was the feeding of the five thousand with five loaves and two fishes (Matthew 14:16-20). An up-to-date example also comes to mind.

When I was first converted there was a dear lady who took me under her wing and prayed for me. That's a very scriptural way to deal with young converts. She was an elderly woman on a very limited income. Since the day of her conversion she had learned to trust God for everything, and her faith was a great inspiration.

I remember going to her house one day when she had just come home from being out witnessing for the Lord, and a parcel was delivered from one of the big stores in the city.

On the parcel it simply said, "From the Lord Jesus Christ." It was a brand new coat, and she had been praying for a coat. I asked her, "Aren't you going to try it on to see if it fits?" She looked at me reproachfully and said, "Don, I don't have to do that; the Lord knows my size!"

Now this same woman had a very strict belief about not working or shopping on Sundays. She lived alone and one day a car load of people turned up for Sunday tea. All she had in the house was a small part of a loaf of bread and some butter. What should she do?

Immediately, she prayed, "Lord, it's Sunday and I'm not going to the shop to buy anything." Then she laid her hands on that little piece of bread and continued, "Lord, I want You to multiply this bread like You did the loaves and fishes by Galilee."

Then, by faith, she began to cut slices of bread and butter, and she filled a great plateful. When she had finished, the piece of bread was still the same size as when she had started! That is the gift of the working of miracles! If God couldn't do that, He wouldn't be God.

Other good examples of non-healing miracles are the series of miracles the Lord performed through Moses before Pharoah would let the Hebrew nation go (Exodus, chapters seven through twelve); and of course there is the parting of the Red Sea so that they could cross on dry land.

In the New Testament there is the example of the Lord sending Peter to get the coin out of the fish's mouth (Matthew 17:24-27). It's certainly not the normal thing for fish to swim around with coins in their mouths. But the Lord sent Peter, and there was the fish and there was the coin, and the taxes were paid.

You can find numerous other non-healing miracles in the pages of the Old and New Testament. And the Lord has provided miracle after miracle for us too in the Good News Crusade ministry. He is "the same yesterday, and today, and for ever" (Hebrews 13:8).

CHAPTER 8

THE GIFT OF PROPHECY

Its Purpose

"... to another prophecy"

Prophecy is a wonderful gift. It is actually God speaking through a human channel. We need to recognize this and to reverence the gift as something very precious. It so often happens that when a prophecy is given in a meeting, we go home and forget and take no action on it—yet it was *God speaking to us!*

I believe the more we respect prophecy, the more we act upon what God says to us, the deeper this gift will go in the church. One of the most important factors in moving out into the realm of prophecy is that we put a proper value on it.

Now the gift of prophecy is not to be confused with the ministry of a prophet. In Ephesians 4:11 we find the ministry gifts of the ascended Lord—apostles, prophets, evangelists, pastors and teachers. But the gift of prophecy is something different in that *all* the members of the Body of Christ may prophesy. That doesn't mean they all have the ministry of a prophet.

The ministry of a prophet could bring guidance to us and can reveal future events. But the gift of prophecy will never give guidance, although I do believe it can in some way confirm guidance already received.

First Corinthians 14:3 tells us clearly for what purpose the gift of prophecy is given, "He that prophesieth speaketh unto men to edification, and exhortation, and comfort."

Now, whatever we do in the realm of the Spirit must be in the context of the Word of God. It doesn't matter what excuses people make for going beyond that boundary. God never speaks outside of what the Bible can back up. And I believe the gift of prophecy will never operate outside these three realms given to us in the written Word of God—edification, exhortation, and comfort.

Edification

You will find the word edify used often as Paul writes to the churches. Going back to the Greek, it means, "to build up or improve." The church desperately needs edifying and so it desperately needs the gift of prophecy. When we see what the gifts are supposed to do and recognize the need for them, it will draw these ministries out of us.

Since prophecy then is to edify, build up, to improve, it doesn't go around knocking people down, smashing them to pieces, bringing them into bondage and condemnation. In fact, the opposite is true. God's prophecy releases people from these things. Prophecy is to build up, to improve, to encourage, to express to us the provision of God, to give us a vision of what He has for us.

Exhortation

Exhortation means "to incite by words or advice, to encourage, warn or caution." It may include a rebuke, it is true, but it is not just a cold, dry, callous rebuke. Exhortation shows what is wrong and then gives the answer for it. Hallelujah! It was used in this way once in my own life.

A certain sin took hold of me some years ago, and no matter how I tried, I couldn't seem to get the victory. So I sank into the vicious old circle—sinned, repented, came back and did it again; sinned, repented, came back and did it again. This went on for weeks, and I knew it was not pleasing to the Lord.

One day I went into a meeting and sat in the back row. Nobody knew I was there at that point, as it was in another city, and no one knew anything about me or my condition. I had not been there many minutes when a sister stood up and began to prophesy. She said something like this:

"You are going round and round in circles. All you are doing is going round and round in circles and coming back to the same place every time. You are sinning and repenting, sinning and repenting. You are going around the bottom of a mountain. That is why you are always coming back to the same place."

Then, after the rebuke, came the answer for my freedom.

"You must turn and face the mountain. Come to Me with your problem, and I will lift you up and put you on top of the mountain."

Right then and there that is what I did, and God met me, hallelujah!

Doesn't the Word tell us that when we prophesy the

secrets of men's hearts will be revealed (1 Corinthians 14:24-25)? But let me repeat—it is not to condemn. Jesus did not come into the world to condemn, but that the world through Him might be saved (John 3:17).

When somebody says to me, "I have this gift and the Lord has shown me such and such about a certain person," I take note. I know I need to watch and be careful, because this brother or sister isn't truly moving in the Spirit. There's a kink; there's something wrong. God reveals things through prophecy or one of the other gifts only to bring the answer—to see a need met.

Comfort

Oh, how much the Body of Christ needs comforting! Human sympathy is a poor substitute for God's comfort. Wouldn't it be wonderful if whenever we met together, first one, then another, and then another would prophesy? The word would go deep into people's hearts and comfort them. It's so easy in this world to get discouraged. Not that I am making excuses for people getting discouraged, defeated and depressed. Jesus has provided a perfect victory so that discouragement is not necessary. But it doesn't alter the fact that it happens.

I have yet to be in a company of the Lord's people to minister and not find anyone who needed comforting. I believe if the gift of prophecy was operating correctly, and efficiently, and sufficiently, we wouldn't need a line of people coming to be counseled, conference after conference, meeting after meeting, when itinerant ministries are passing through. The gift of prophecy in their local church would have met those needs when the people first began to get down. The word of the Lord would have come, revealed their hearts, comforted and lifted them up.

There was an occasion in my own life when this ministry was such a relief. I had something which the devil would always use to condemn me, something from my distant past which he would constantly dig up, particularly if we were in the midst of a spiritual battle. That would be the time the enemy would be sure to find someone to use to harass me. They'd write me a letter. Or there would be a phone call. Or someone would come and tell me, "Do you know what so and so said about you?"

In those days, there was only one way I could get any comfort. I'd go into my room, get on my knees with my Bible and search the Scriptures. And the Scriptures would begin to comfort me.

On this particular day, several years ago, I had experienced the usual barrage, and felt myself going down and down. I went into my bedroom, fell on my knees and began to search the Scriptures. While I was doing this, someone came to the house. I'd only seen this person once before, and he knew nothing about my situation.

I was called out of the room and we began to have some fellowship. We'd only just started when my visitor said, "Let's have a time of prayer." No sooner had we begun to pray when this dear brother came over to me, laid his hands on me, and began to prophesy. And these were his words:

"Go not into thy room to get on thy knees and search the Scriptures on this matter again, because I have forgiven thee. Thy complete past is under My precious blood. Thou art forgiven. Thou art My child. Thou art

My servant."

Well, as you can imagine, the devil couldn't even *begin* to try to condemn me on that again. It brought permanent comfort to my heart.

And what a joy it is to be used in such a ministry as prophecy. There's so much criticism, and backbiting, and breaking down in our churches. How beautiful it is to be used to bring a message of comfort to the Lord's people.

CHAPTER 9

THE GIFT OF PROPHECY

You May All Prophesy

Now we need to consider the question: Who may prophesy and how many?

First Corinthians 14:31 tells us, "For ye may all prophesy one by one, that all may learn, and all may be comforted." When you are prophesying, people are learning and people are comforted—so you may *all* prophesy.

I believe that if we are baptized in the Holy Spirit we should believe and expect God to use us in the gift of prophecy. This is one gift we should all covet (1 Corinthians 14:39). If the Bible says we should all prophesy and you haven't yet done so, then it's time you sought the Lord and began.

There is a church in a certain city, which I visit quite often, where you can guarantee there will be at least twelve to twenty prophecies in every meeting. The service starts at eleven o'clock on a Sunday morning, but if you get there at a quarter to eleven, you have really missed half the meeting. When they come together they don't wait for someone to stand up in the front and say, "Now we'll sing hymn 320." They start praising the Lord on their own. And it isn't long before someone prophesies.

There is a certain principal of a Bible school who goes to that church, and he sits there and writes down all the prophecies. I've heard him say, "I never need to prepare a sermon, because God always gives me my sermon points through the prophecies." I'm not sure whether or not that's the right way to get a sermon! But I do know that church has had permanent revival for thirty-five years.

On one occasion, some students came from another Bible college where they had been taught that you can only have a few prophecies in a meeting. They had literally come to criticize—to investigate how it should not be done.

Now, nobody knew anything about them at that stage. They came in and sat in the back row. But it wasn't long before a string of prophecies came along this line: *"You have come and you have bricks in your pocket to throw..."* and the prophecies began to describe the attitudes of these young people. Afterwards the students came and repented, confessing to the pastor, "God spoke to us before we could do anything."

You see, if the gift of prophecy is operating properly, people can't come in and ruin the meeting through negative resentments and criticism. Provided we are moving correctly in the Spirit, we may all prophesy. Even some of the weaker members of the Body of Christ should be prophesying. The most elementary Christian can be used in this gift.

Naturally, the deeper we go with God, the deeper the gift of prophecy will become. I am not advocating that it remain on a shallow level. But I want us to see from the Scripture that no one is barred.

In 1 Corinthians 12:22-24 we read, "On the contrary, it is much truer that the members of the body which seem to be weaker are necessary; and those members of the body, which we deem less honorable, on these we bestow more abundant honor, and our unseemly members come to have more abundant seemliness, whereas our seemly members have no need of it. But God has so composed the body, giving more abundant honor to that member which lacked..." (*NASB*). So when you look around and see people upon whom you might be tempted to look down, thinking they aren't "spiritual" enough to prophesy, remember God has given more abundant honor to them.

Now, if we could only encourage everyone, and love everyone, and bring all into the realm of the gifts of the Spirit, we should find God speaking through these people in a mighty way.

These uncomely parts are very vital, for when the uncomely parts of the Body of Christ are not functioning properly, the Church does not appear very beautiful.

You would never find a man who is in love with a woman saying, "Darling, what beautiful kidneys you have!" or "I just adore your liver!" Yet, they are just as important as her eyes. If those kidneys and liver are not functioning properly, that young lady will not look very charming at all. Her complexion will be horrible. In fact, the kidneys and liver are essential to her very life.

This is what these verses are talking about—the

uncomely parts, the parts that lack. These are the ones we should be encouraging to function in the Body of Christ. "You may *all* prophesy one by one."

CHAPTER 10

THE GIFT OF PROPHECY

How To Prophesy

Now we come to the question: *How do we prophesy?*
Romans 12:6 tells us, "Having then gifts differing according to the grace that is given to us, whether prophecy, let us prophesy according to the proportion of faith."

A Spirit-filled person with faith in his heart can prophesy. It doesn't matter whether the prophecy is long or short. Don't be put off by someone who can stand and prophesy for twenty minutes, or by those who have a lovely fluent tongue. You prophesy according to the proportion of your faith. If you can only bring a sentence—bring it. That could be the very key that will unlock the whole meeting. Some of the little tiny prophecies are among the best I have ever heard.

Quite often, the gifts seem to operate in the wrong place in a meeting. Someone will come into a service stewing up inside to give a prophecy. They know the Spirit of the Lord is on them and they have a prophecy to give. But they wait, and wait, and the meeting proceeds, and before long the preacher is preaching.

While the minister is giving his message, the person with the prophecy thinks, "Well, it really is from the Lord, because that's exactly what He's given me." After the sermon, out comes the prophecy, confirming the word that has been preached. But it would have been far better if that prophecy had been given before the sermon, encouraging the preacher, confirming to him that he had the word of the Lord, and introducing the word into the meeting.

Some of the best meetings I have been in have started with the gift of prophecy, before there was a hymn or a chorus, or a note played on the piano, or before anybody prayed. I believe the earlier in the meeting the prophecies come the better. So be sensitive to the Lord. You don't have to wait for a lovely "spiritual" atmosphere before you prophesy. If you come to a meeting and God has laid something on your spirit, just ask the Lord, "When should it be?" and quite often you will find it is "Now," or near the beginning of the meeting.

Sometimes one person will start prophesying, and another will come in with a bit more of the prophecy, and another one will follow, and we begin to get a picture of what God wants for that particular gathering. By the way, He doesn't want it exactly like the last one. God has a tremendous variety. So we prophesy according to the proportion of our faith.

In James 2:17-19 we read; "Even so faith, if it has no works, is dead, being by itself. But someone may well say, 'You have faith, and I have works; show me your faith without the works, and I will show you my faith by my works.' You believe that God is one. You do well; the demons also believe, and shudder" (*NASB*).

What this literally means is: If you say, "I've got faith, I believe," but don't do anything to show it, you are in no better position than the devil. He believes in God. He believes in Jesus Christ. The devil believes in the gifts of the Spirit, the gift of prophecy, miracles, signs and wonders. He knows all about them. But of course he's not committed to them—if he was he'd be converted!

You may say, "Oh, I believe in the gifts of the Spirit. I believe in the gift of prophecy." That doesn't mean a thing. James says, "Show me your faith *without* your works" (and *that's* a challenge because it's impossible) "and I will show you my faith *by* my works." Paraphrased that means, "I'll show you what I believe by what I produce."

And this is what God truly desires from the Body of Christ—to show the world what it believes by what it produces. This is what God wants of us in the gift of prophecy. I believe the operation of the gift of prophecy is one of the most practical ways that we can show our faith, because it is one of the works of faith. So, we must have faith in order to prophesy, but we need to work our faith. And there is only one way to do that—how? The answer is in Galatians 5:6 ". . . faith which worketh by love."

Faith and love—these are the two major keys to unlock the gift of prophecy. We prophesy according to the proportion of our faith, but it takes love to work our faith. First Corinthians 13:13 reads, "And now abideth faith, hope, love, these three; but the greatest of these is love" (*NASB*).

Why is love greater than faith and hope?

Bible hope is a relation of faith. It is not the weak

sentimental word we have in this twentieth century. Hope in its original meaning was a *certainty*. If today you say "I hope,..." you mean "maybe." Originally it meant "will be."

Hope is "future faith." Faith is for now. But hope is a certainty for the future. The Bible tells us that we are saved by hope (Romans 8:24). In other words, I am absolutely certain God is going to keep me and get me home to glory in the future. That is my "blessed hope." So you can put hope and faith together and make them one. Present and future faith.

Now why is love greater than faith? Faith is that spiritual faculty by which we *receive* something from God. But love always *gives*. I believe the reason love is greater than faith is because "it is more blessed to give than to receive" (Acts 20:35 *NASB*).

The Bible doesn't say love is *better* than faith. It says it is *greater*. If I have faith I can receive all I need and stack it up. But if I have faith and *love*, I can obtain all that is needed and then *give it away*—and that is greater. This, I believe, is the whole principle on which the gift of prophecy operates.

I need a proportion of faith to *get* a word from the Lord for the Body of Christ assembled at a particular time, or perhaps for a member of that Body—and I need to have love to *give* it to them. The fact that I have love moves me to use my faith. In other words, *my love for the Body of Christ works my faith*. If you love me, you want to edify me, to exhort and comfort me. And if I love you, I want to edify, exhort and comfort you.

We're told to love our neighbors as ourselves. I love myself an awful lot! And I'm trying to love myself more so that I can love my neighbor more! The more I love myself, the more I love you, because we are in the same body. I don't love my hands more than I love my feet. And if I'm a hand and you're a foot, we must love each other the same. Didn't Jesus say, "Inasmuch as ye have done it unto the least of these my brethren, ye have done it unto me" (Matthew 25:40)? He is the Head, and I believe we have to love the Body of Christ like we love the Head. If we do—then we are going to prophesy.

Now don't say you can't. God says you *can*. All you have to do is start loving someone. I find it so easy to love the Lord's people. Don't you? If not, there's something wrong. You see, the gift of prophecy is only getting something from God that He wants to give and then delivering it. Delivery boy—that's all you are!

The Bible says, ". . . desire spiritual gifts, but rather that ye may prophesy" (1 Corinthians 14:1). In the Greek, the word desire is a very strong one. It literally means "to track it down." I don't think we can just dismiss the gift of prophecy and say, "Oh, Lord, if You want to give it to me, I'll have it." But rather, we have to go after it, and desire it, and not give up until it is operating effectively in our lives and ministries.

How do I know I have a prophecy from God?

In our chapter on the word of knowledge, we dealt with the problem of the one who is always wondering, "Is it from me, is it from the Lord? Is it from the devil?" I said then, and I repeat now, *God can only speak to faith.*

I believe Romans 8:16 gives us the answer to this problem. "The Spirit itself beareth witness with our spirit, that we are the children of God." People call this "the witness of the Spirit." Of course, it is usually associated with the assurance of salvation. But in the very same way you know you are saved, so you can also know when you have a prophecy from the Lord. There will be a witness. There may be some heart pounding and joyful excitement that God is about to use you, but there will still be a settled peace in your spirit.

Judging prophecy

The gift of prophecy has to be judged. "Let the prophets speak two or three, and let the other judge" (1 Corinthians 14:29). Prophecy has to be judged in the sense of assessing what has been said.

There are times when there might be quite a long prophecy and just one sentence in it is for me, and one for you, and one for someone else. If we all tried to make each part apply in our lives, we could be confused or disappointed. You just don't take everything that is said through the gift of prophecy as being personally for you. You assess it in the Spirit.

We also need to assess it in the light of the Word of God. Is it scriptural? It may not be Scripture, but as long as it is scriptural it is perfectly all right.

Divine co-operation

Finally, 1 Corinthians 14:32 tells us, "The spirits of the prophets are subject to the prophets." This is a tremendous principle that I want to bring home very forcibly.

God doesn't put your personality aside when you prophesy. God will never possess you in the sense of making you do something against your will. The spirit of the prophet is subject to the prophet. The whole realm of the Spirit is divine co-operation, between His Spirit and your spirit. "He that is joined unto the Lord is one spirit" (1 Corinthians 6:17).

It's like getting married. Two persons become one flesh. But a lot of married couples live like two individuals, and those marriages are never a success. But when two persons are made one, and learn to live like one, then that is a beautiful, happy marriage. And it's the same in the realm of the Spirit.

You can have the Holy Spirit, and yet be living like two individuals—your spirit and the Holy Spirit living differently. It takes co-operation to live as one spirit. Just as marriage can only work successfully on the ground of submission, so in the realm of the Spirit.

If you say "No" to the Holy Spirit, you grieve Him, but He won't force you. However, as you submit to Him, you flow together in divine cooperation—and it's beautiful.

May I also say that the Holy Spirit can speak twentieth century English? After all, why should He speak sixteenth century English? Why not first century if we insist it must be the old stuff? Now, I'm not criticizing anyone. I tend to speak sixteenth century English too when I prophesy. I just say this for those who don't prophesy in what I call KJV language.

Some people prophesy in RSV. Some people now prophesy in Living Bible language. I've never heard anyone prophesy in Amplified yet—because they can't put in the brackets! It might sound funny, but it's helpful to see this. Whatever way we are conversant with the Bible is likely to be the way the prophecy will come over. Let's be free to allow the Holy Spirit to speak in our natural language, the supernatural words He wants to say to us.

And let's not just sit back and leave it to the person

next to us to prophesy. If we do, we'll be robbing ourselves, and probably someone else as well. There are areas where one person may not be able to "get through" to a certain other person. But God has someone in the Body of Christ who can. And it may be you!

CHAPTER 11

DISCERNING OF SPIRITS

"... to another discerning of spirits"

This is a very important gift, and for a pastor, one of the best gifts to covet. Please notice first of all it is a "discerning of spirits," not a discerning of what people are thinking and doing. I've had people come up to me and say, "Reverend Double, I have the gift of discernment." And they begin to relate something that has nothing to do with spirits. Then I begin to wonder about the source of the supposed gift. Certainly it is not a gift of the Holy Spirit.

The gift under discussion is a gift of "discerning of spirits." And when it operates it is not to afford you the opportunity of running around saying, "This person has an unclean spirit," or "That person has a jealous spirit." Every time these gifts operate, it is to enable you to minister to the one concerned, either bringing deliverance or setting him on the road to deliverance.

The servant of God needs discernment for three types of spirits. The first one to notice is the human spirit.

First Thessalonians 5:23 reads, "...I pray God your whole spirit and soul and body be preserved blameless...."

Also, Hebrews 4:12, "The word of God is quick, and powerful, and sharper than any two-edged sword, piercing even to the dividing asunder of soul and spirit...." The Word of God alone can divide between soul and spirit, but it's important to see that there is a division. Two different parts of our individual make-up.

The human spirit, I believe, is that part of us which is born again. Our souls are saved. But it is our spirits that are born from above. I do not believe that they are in any way interchangeable. And when you see the difference and understand the Scriptures, you come to a place where you are much more able to help people.

Another reason for being able to discern a human spirit is because sometimes in a meeting a very enthusiastic human spirit will manifest itself, and we need to be able to discern the difference between that and the Holy Spirit and correct these dear people.

Sometimes, even so-called prophecies come out of the human spirit. They are not necessarily in error, they may be clearly scriptural, but the important thing is that they are not a part of God's program for that meeting. If you have the ministry of pastor or elder, you, especially, need to ask God for the gift of discerning of spirits so that you may intervene.

The next spirit we must consider is, of course, the Holy Spirit. It is important to be able to discern the movement of the Holy Spirit, even as we mentioned above.

There is a pastor in Kansas City, Kansas, who learned

what it was to keenly discern the Holy Spirit, and I would like to share his experience with you.

This pastor left home one Saturday morning to perform a wedding service under very trying circumstances. The relatives of the young couple hated each other and actually had threatened violence the night before at the wedding rehearsal. As he left the house his wife prayed, "Lord, guide him today in the discerning of spirits." Naturally, this pastor thought that he would be in spiritual warfare with evil spirits that day. But instead, he found himself just following the Holy Spirit's direction in every detail of the day, what sermon to preach, what prayers to pray.

And as the day progressed, this pastor discovered a marvelous thing. As he followed the guidance of the Holy Spirit, he didn't need to come against any unholy spirits. The Lord's anointing was there, the tension among the families was broken, and his wife's prayer was answered in an unexpected way. The spirit he had needed to discern that day was the Holy Spirit and Him alone! Hallelujah, there was great victory that day!

Then, of course, the third kind of spirits are evil spirits. When it comes to evil spirits, I do not believe a truly born-again Christian can be possessed, but I do believe that in the soul realm, that is in the realm of the mind, will and emotions, they can be bound by evil spirits.

Now I'd like to say a little about demon power. If you don't agree with me, I hope you'll still love me. I think there is a good deal of excessive teaching which gives the devil a lot of glory he doesn't deserve. Many things the devil and demons are blamed for are nothing more than the soulish realm of man.

One of the reasons for the confusion is that man has tried to split up the realm of demon activity into possession and oppression, depression and obsession.

In the Greek there is only one word, "demonized." This word is important. To me it simply means that the condition of this person, no matter how slight or severe, is a result of demon activity. It doesn't matter to me how the demon is active. He has to obey me when I speak in Jesus' name and order him to go.

Remember Mark 16:17 tells us to cast out demons, not coax them out. And we don't need an intellectual appreciation of what is really going on in order to know it is the devil and to tell him to go. The Lord has given us this authority through His death on the cross.

I remember very early in my ministry being taught an important lesson. A man was brought into a meeting drunk. It was very obvious there were evil spirits at work. I went with another minister into a little room to pray for his deliverance, and I was ready to roll up my sleeves and have a real long session. You see, I had read some of the books about oppression, possession, etc., which had given me a very firm impression that it was more difficult to deliver someone possessed than one merely oppressed. It's amazing how books condition one's thinking.

The other brother just walked in and prayed. He rebuked the devil, told him to go, turned round and walked out of the room. The man looked no better at all so I went running after the minister saying, "Aren't you going to wrestle and really get this man through?" He replied, "Don, I have received what I prayed for," and went on his way. The drunk man went home.

The next evening, this same man was back in the

meeting. He was gloriously saved, and was soon baptized in water. Not long afterwards, he was baptized in the Holy Spirit. This is the authority God has given us!

The devil will give you a performance of all his tricks as long as you allow him to do it. When it comes to talking and having conversations with demons, they will keep you talking all night if you let them. But Jesus would never put up with that. He said, "Hold your peace, and come out." That's authority. Let's please remember that, and not get caught up with the frill and fancies. Let's get the job done!

In the deliverance ministry, as in every phase of the Christian walk, it is of utmost importance to be led by the Spirit. If you will remember, in an earlier chapter the Lord told me *not* to cast demons out of an unsaved man because he would be worse off than he was before. But in this case with the drunken man, by the Sovreignty of God, the Lord knew the man was ready for deliverance *and* for salvation, so He led us to cast out the demons.

Also, in the deliverance ministry, it is very important to have the discerning of spirits. One of the big advantages is that it enables you to name the evil spirits. Mark 9:25-27 is an example from the ministry of the Lord Jesus.

"When Jesus saw that the people came running together, he rebuked the foul spirit saying unto him (notice the spirit is a 'him'—it's a personality and Jesus named it), Thou deaf and dumb spirit, I charge thee, come out of him, and enter no more into him. And the spirit cried, and rent him sore, and came out of him: and he was as one dead; insomuch that many said, He is dead. But Jesus took him by the hand, and lifted him up; and he arose."

A model deliverance! No fuss, no bother!

We find another example in Acts 16:16-18. I mention this one again to prove it was not only the Lord Jesus who could deal with demons. Paul cast out a spirit of divination from a slave girl who was a soothsayer, a fortuneteller.

There is a tremendous increase of this in the world today. A real fortuneteller is controlled by an evil spirit, and believe me it's not something that can be lightly ignored. One of the problems is that the church has been ignorant of the power that these spirits can have in people's lives.

I think I could say without exaggeration that we have met literally hundreds of persons who were unable to receive the baptism in the Holy Spirit, until we discovered they had been to a fortuneteller. They first had to be delivered and then they were filled.

Even reading horoscopes can bring you into terrible bondage. God showed me it is like this: The Word of God is described as the seed of God. When we receive it into our lives it grows and bears fruit. That is even how we are converted. A horoscope or the prophecy of a fortuneteller is like a seed of the devil. It is planted in the heart where it grows and produces bondage.

In my own life, as a young man, I went to a fortuneteller. Later, when I heard a minister speak on the need of deliverance, I thought, "Well, that's ridiculous." Then I said to myself, "I'm a reasonable kind of chap, it won't do any harm to get him to pray for me. If there's anything in it, it will work." Previously, I thought anything like that would have been dealt with at conversion. So I was prayed for, and I can truthfully say there was a tremendous release in my life.

Up until that time, the fortuneteller's predictions had brought fears and bondages into my life. From the moment of prayer, I couldn't even remember what the fortuneteller had said. If I think of the occasion, my mind just seems to be filled with thinking about the blood of the Lord Jesus Christ. So, I found out that it really did work.

Another time, I was at a conference and a certain minister, feeling an anointing of the Spirit, came over to pray for me. He said, "Don, I discern there is an inferiority-complex spirit in you." Now, he would never pray for anyone unless the person admitted what he said was true. He asked, "Is that right, Don?"

I was on the spot. I had never heard of an inferiority-complex spirit! But I was honest with myself, and I knew that I did have a huge inferiority-complex, so I said, "Yes, brother." He prayed for me and rebuked the spirit and cast it out. I've never been bound by it from that day to this! Before I had thought my feelings of inferiority were a virtue, a part of being humble!

I want to tell you, such a change took place in my life that I hardly recognize myself now. I used to just sit in a corner out of sight. If there was anyone else who could minister or speak, I wouldn't open my mouth. But now it doesn't matter who's around. If I am on the same platform as outstanding preachers, it makes no difference to me, because I realize this: the Holy Spirit in me is the same as the Holy Spirit in anyone else.

If you are relying on your intellectual ability, or on what you know, then you can compare yourself with other people and feel inferior. But if you are relying on the Holy Spirit and what *He* knows, then there is no one with whom to make a comparison.

In any event, I do believe the devil was responsible for my complex, and since my deliverance, I have shared this with many and have seen others delivered of the same thing.

Finally, in the discerning of spirits, John tells us to "... try the spirits whether they are of God" (1 John 4:1). That is a command. We don't just accept everybody and everything they say. We need to try the spirits, and there are times when only the discerning of spirits can give the answer.

One other thing on discerning spirits I have observed: the Lord Jesus came in flesh and blood and there is one thing evil spirits dislike above all else—the blood of Jesus Christ.

There have been times when I have been dealing with people possessed with evil spirits, and witches, and I began to mention the blood of Jesus. They've snarled at me like a dog, saying, "Don't mention that blood here." The Holy Spirit will always exalt the blood of Jesus that was shed for our redemption. Evil spirits will reject it. The devil hates the blood of Jesus because: "They overcame him (Satan) by the blood of the Lamb, and by the word of their testimony..." (Revelation 12:11).

Satan is defeated!

CHAPTER 12

TONGUES AND INTERPRETATION

A Valuable Gift

"...to another divers kinds of tongues, to another the interpretation of tongues"

We now come to the last two gifts, "divers kinds of tongues" and "the interpretation of tongues." In the Bible, there are four main reasons for speaking in tongues, and one of them is accompanied by the final gift of the Spirit, "interpretation of tongues." But the first reason the Bible reveals for speaking in tongues is as evidence of the baptism in the Holy Spirit.

Tongues as evidence

We find this in Acts 2:4, "And they were all filled with the Holy Ghost, and began to speak with other tongues, as the Spirit gave them utterance." Here the Scriptures show that speaking in other tongues is definitely an evidence of being baptized with the Holy Spirit. Other records of this happening in the Bible include when the house of Cornelius (Acts 10:44-46) and the men of Ephesus (Acts 19:6) began speaking with other tongues as soon as the Spirit came upon them.

Now I believe that everyone who is baptized in the Holy Spirit *can* speak in tongues. Whether they do or not is another matter. Some say, "Well, can't the Lord manifest another gift to give us evidence that we're baptized with the Holy Spirit?" That is an age-old excuse because some people do not want to speak in tongues.

There were approximately one hundred and twenty people in the upper room on the day of Pentecost, and the Bible says that every one of them began to speak in other tongues, when they were filled with the Holy Spirit. If other gifts needed to be manifested to give evidence they were Spirit-filled, I'm sure the Lord would have divided them out there.

Now, it is certainly true that as we continue on in our Spirit-filled lives, and as we are "being continuously filled with the Spirit" (as the literal Greek reads in Ephesians 5:18), there are other evidences of leading a Spirit-filled life.

Acts 1:8 says, "You shall receive power when the Holy Spirit has come upon you" (*NASB*). There should be some power in our lives! The Bible also says that the Holy Spirit will show us the things of Christ, making the Lord Jesus more real to us (John 16:13-15).

First John 2:27 tells us that the anointing teaches us all things. In other words, the Holy Spirit will make the Bible more real to us. Romans 5:5 reads, "The love of God is shed in our hearts by the Holy Ghost." There should be a new dimension of love in our lives.

But even if these things are apparent, I've never met anyone who has been satisfied he was Spirit-filled until he has spoken in tongues. Biblically, there is something speaking in tongues does for you that nothing else can do. So firstly, speaking in tongues is one of the evidences of being filled with the Holy Spirit.

Tongues for interpretation

The second use of speaking in tongues is "the gift of tongues" to the church. It is when the gift of tongues is used in this way that the final gift of the Spirit, "the interpretation of tongues," is used, and it is a very valuable gift.

Although every Spirit-filled believer can speak in tongues, they only have the manifestation of tongues as *the gift to the church* when the Holy Spirit chooses (1 Corinthians 12:11).

First Corinthians 12:29-30 asks, "Are all apostles?" Obviously not! The Bible says that God gave *some* as apostles (Ephesians 4:11).

"Are all prophets?" Again the answer is "no," otherwise we'd all be living in the future. "Are all teachers?" I'm certainly glad we're not all teachers or we'd have spiritual indigestion!

"Are all workers of miracles?" Again the answer is definitely "no." "Have all the gifts of healing?" The answer is still "no." "Do all speak with tongues?" In the context here, the answer is a decided "no." But we must see the setting in which this is written. Paul is talking about ministry in the church. This is tongues for interpretation.

I believe one of the major uses of this gift in the church is when a meeting is dead and flat. But if a meeting is flowing in the blessing of God, prophecy is more appropriate.

One of the reasons a meeting becomes flat and dry is

because people are not responding to the Lord. Their minds are wandering all over the place. They're thinking of what they are going to have for supper, or about granny they left at home, or perhaps what they are going to do at business the next day. This causes the meeting to be very flat.

I don't believe it is ever God's will for us to have a dead, flat meeting. But when it has become that way, it's an ideal opportunity for the gifts of tongues and interpretation to operate. For when we speak in tongues for interpretation, it is not to show off, it is to alert the congregation that God is speaking from heaven.

So with the meeting flat, and people's minds wandering all over the place, someone is anointed and speaks in other tongues. What happens? Immediately, everyone's attention is brought to the Lord. And somebody stands and gives the interpretation so that everyone can understand the message from God. Every thought is brought into captivity to the obedience of Christ, and you feel the meeting begin to lift. And it flows on in the blessing of God.

Another use of the gifts of tongues and interpretation in the church is to change the course of a meeting. Even Spirit-filled Christians tend to get into ruts. We find that people come along to a service, and have a hymn and a prayer, another hymn and a Bible reading, and another hymn and a testimony, another hymn and take up the offering, give out the notices, another hymn and a message, another hymn and go home. And this goes on week after week.

Some churches I go to, I can tell you in advance what's going to happen because that was the way they did it last time I was there. They have it all nicely written out. And I'm sure God is looking down from heaven and thinking, "I'd like to have a little change."

Then one day someone gets anointed and in the middle of it all speaks with tongues. And the interpretation gives direction from God for the meeting to take a different course. It's really wonderful when that happens.

Personally, I believe that every meeting should be different as we look to the Holy Spirit for His direction. On one occasion, I had been introduced to speak at a meeting, and the Lord still hadn't given me a message. So I just stood up in faith and began to chat. After about five minutes the message came and we had a wonderful time.

We need to be entirely open to the Holy Spirit to change the course of our meetings. And the gifts of the Spirit are very valuable to do this. Especially tongues and interpretation.

A sign for unbelievers
The third use of the gift of tongues is in 1 Corinthians 14:22, "Wherefore tongues are for a sign, not to them that believe, but to them that believe not." One famous translator of the Bible actually believed that the Scriptures made a mistake here. He said he was sure the writer meant that tongues were for believers. He forgot there are a great many *unbelieving believers*.

An unbelieving believer is a person who is saved— washed in the blood of Jesus—but has said, "So far and no further. I don't think God can give me anything more than I have." An unbelieving believer is a person who says, "I don't believe in the baptism in the Holy Spirit. I don't believe in speaking in tongues."An unbelieving believer is a person who says, "I don't believe miracles are for today." The gift of tongues is a sign to such.

A friend of mine was in a meeting in an Anglican church in England where the Holy Spirit was moving. Present in the meeting was the German editor of a Christian periodical, who at that time did not believe in the baptism in the Spirit. During the service, the Spirit of the Lord came upon my friend and he spoke out in tongues. But he was puzzled because no one followed with the interpretation.

Immediately following the meeting, the German editor went up to my friend and said, "Where did you learn that beautiful German?"

"I don't know any German," my friend replied. "I've never spoken German in my life. All I know is I was speaking in tongues."

"But you were speaking the most beautiful, correct German I have ever heard and were asking God to take your life and use you," said the editor.

"Well, brother, that's the result of the baptism in the Holy Spirit," my friend answered.

Immediately the German brother responded, "Then I want it. Will you please pray for me." And he was filled with the Spirit and spoke with tongues on the spot. That was a case where the gift of tongues was used as a sign to an unbelieving believer.

An excellent example of the effect of tongues on actual unbelievers was on the day of Pentecost. This is also another case where the gift of interpretation wasn't needed. The disciples received the evidence of the baptism by speaking in tongues in the upper room. Then they went into the streets of Jerusalem and spoke with tongues. And Jerusalem certainly wasn't filled with believers. It was full of unbelievers.

As they went into the streets speaking in tongues, the people who were there from many parts of the world heard these disciples speaking of the wonderful works of God; and each heard in his own native tongue which the speaker had never learned. As a result of speaking in tongues and Peter's preaching, three thousand souls were saved. Yet some people say tongues have no value.

On another occasion, a friend of mine from South Africa went to speak to a tribe. When he arrived, the whole tribe had assembled, but they waited in vain for the interpreter to turn up. My friend didn't know a word in the tribal dialect, so he prayed and asked the Lord what to do. Then he felt the anointing of the Spirit coming upon him, and he stood and began to speak in tongues.

To his amazement and joy, he realized he was obviously preaching in the tribal language, and as he came towards the end of his message, the natives were all coming forward and kneeling around him. The outcome was the entire tribe was converted to the Lord including the chief. That was the gift of tongues as a sign. A very valuable gift indeed!

CHAPTER 13

TONGUES

For Private Edification

The fourth and final use of tongues is found in 1 Corinthians 14:4, "He that speaketh in an unknown tongue edifieth himself." If we are honest, we'll all admit that we need edifying. The Bible tells us when we speak in tongues we edify ourselves. Of course, this is in our own private devotions. This is between God and ourselves alone.

We touched on the meaning of the word "edify" when we dealt with the gift of prophecy. J. B. Phillips translating verse four says, "He that speaks in an unknown tongue builds himself up." How we need to build ourselves up! I need building up every day, and several times during the day. In the ability we have to speak in tongues, we have a tremendous potential within us to build ourselves up.

The Amplified Bible translates the same verse, "He who speaks in a [strange] tongue . . . improves himself." I'm sure every one of us would be willing to admit there is room for improvement. People from certain denominational churches have sometimes said for

81

instance, "We're Baptists; if we get baptized in the Spirit do we have to leave the Baptists and become Pentecostals?" The answer is, "No, not unless the Lord leads, but it *will* make you a better Baptist!" And the same goes for every other Christian denomination, because when you speak in another tongue it improves you.

The apostle Paul puts a tremendous value on this gift. In 1 Corinthians 14:18 he says, "I thank my God, I speak with tongues more than ye all." Paul is actually saying, "Hallelujah! I speak in tongues more than anyone else." He is not belittling the gift, he is magnifying it.

Some people say, "The Bible teaches that tongues is the least of the gifts." I challenge anyone to find it in the Bible and show it to me. I'll tell you before you look. It isn't there. Not only is it not there, it isn't even inferred. You have to absolutely twist Scripture to make a statement like that. And if tongues is considered to be the least simply because it is mentioned last, I have to ask what about faith, hope and love? We can easily see in 1 Corinthians 13:13 that in this list the last mentioned, love, certainly is not the least, but the greatest!

What Paul is saying in 1 Corinthians 14:18 is, "I thank my God I speak with tongues more than you all in my private devotions." Then, in verse 19, he changes the usage and says, "Yet in the church (nothing to do with private devotions) I had rather speak five words with my understanding, that by my voice I might teach others also, than ten thousand words in an unknown tongue."

I say a loud "Amen!" to what Paul said. He is 100 percent right. There is no point in coming to church and just talking in tongues. You could spare yourself the effort of coming.

If people come to church, and all they do is speak in tongues, nobody gets blessed except the person doing the speaking. So Paul gives clear instructions concerning speaking with tongues *in church*. He tells us in verse 13 that if we speak in tongues in church, we should pray that we may interpret.

Yet, Paul is saying that when he did speak in tongues, he thanked God for it, because he did it more than anyone else. I'll put it this way. If the apostle says he spoke in tongues more than anyone else, it's time we tried to catch up. We should put the same value on the gift that the Scriptures indicate Paul did.

What are we doing when we speak in tongues? First Corinthians 14:2 says, "He that speaketh in an unknown tongue speaketh not unto men, but unto God." We're not talking to men. The Bible says we're talking to God.

Isn't that wonderful? When we're speaking with tongues we're speaking to Almighty God. I find that a very awe-inspiring thought. I'm speaking directly to my Creator. No man understand me. I'm in direct personal communion with God in the throne room, and to belittle and criticize that is, I believe, one of the most serious things a Christian can do.

It's so wonderful to me, that I cannot speak with tongues lightly. No one understands it. "Howbeit, in the Spirit he speaketh mysteries" (1 Corinthians 14:2). So I'm not wasting my time or babbling away for no benefit. In the Spirit, I'm speaking mysteries to my Father.

Because we do not have perfect knowledge in many situations, we can pray for our concerns in the Spirit, knowing that we are praying with an understanding beyond our own. If we ever have difficulties with our family, friends or job, we can actually offer up *perfect* prayer to a Father Who hears and answers us!

Secondly, we can pray for situations that we don't even know exist, interceding for those in need or danger of whom we are not aware. There was one Christian man who found out how important that kind of prayer can be. He was praying in the Spirit one morning and found himself in travail as though he had an urgent burden for someone (see Romans 8:26). When his prayer time was over, and he had an assurance that his prayer had been answered, he went off to work, wondering if he would ever know the reason he had prayed so fervently.

Later that day he had his answer. His daughter called him and excitedly explained about an accident that had occurred that morning outside of her apartment. A young six-year-old boy had been struck by a car and thrown fifteen feet. When she reached the child, she found that he was miraculously unharmed.

Imagine the daughter's surprise and the man's joy when they discovered that he had been praying so fervently in the Spirit that morning at the exact time of the accident!

We never know how often our prayers in the Spirit are ones of intercession.

Thirdly, I believe that praying in the Spirit explains some of the differences between the conscious and unconscious mind.

When I pray with my understanding I pray with my

conscious mind about the things I know need prayer. And that is very important. I hope you do plenty of that kind of praying. But there is one thing I cannot do with my conscious mind, and that is pray about the things that are in my subconscious. For I don't know what they are.

I believe the subconscious mind involves the spirit of men, and you will find buried deep down in the spirit of many people things that cause them problems. Tensions, hurts, bitternesses, things that happened years ago; all buried down in the spirit, or subconscious mind.

When psychiatrists psychoanalyze a person, they are trying to unwind and somehow get through to the subconscious mind. They spend hours and hours, years and years, and very often are completely unsuccessful. But God has the answer. We can pray with our spirits.

When we do that, I believe, we release our subconscious mind. As you pray about those tensions, those mental problems, those hurts and those bitternesses that have sunk deep within, you find tremendous relief.

I believe one of the things that goes to one's subconscious is what the medical world calls "shock." My wife and I were in Copenhagen, Denmark, being driven to a meeting by a missionary in a little Fiat car. Our driver went through the traffic lights while they were still red. Unfortunately, another car was coming from the other direction and hit us. I was thrown ten feet into the middle of the road. Cars were whizzing around me from all directions. They picked me up together with my wife and put us in the ambulance. Immediately, we both began to pray in tongues, releasing the shock that was building up inside.

Two men from the church where we were ministering came to the hospital to find out what had happened to us. They asked the ambulance men if there were two English people there. The ambulance attendants replied, "They didn't sound English; they sounded African!" But to cut a long story short, they released us from the hospital that same night. We had been in quite a serious accident, yet had very little shock because we had prayed in the Spirit and the Lord had taken care of our physical needs, releasing the shock within us.

I could tell story after story—amazing illustrations of how the gift of tongues has operated in this way to tremendous spiritual and physical profit. Especially with people who have had mental problems. They have found a release in their spirits they could never find any other way.

Notice, too, the Scriptures say, "I will pray with the Spirit." Paul is not saying, "I *may* do it." He is very firm about it; he says, "I *will* do it." And it's helpful to see that Paul says he will because he could decide *by his own will* to speak "as the Spirit gave the utterance."

In the church, the gift of tongues can only operate *by the will of the Holy Spirit* (1 Corinthians 12:11). But once we've been baptized in the Spirit and received the ability to speak with tongues, we can pray privately with the Spirit whenever *we* so desire.

Paul also says, "I will sing with the spirit, and I will sing with the understanding also" (1 Corinthians 14:15). I will sing with the Spirit—that's a great comfort to some of us who can't sing in tune! This is also a very valuable expression of the gift of tongues.

I am sure many of you have found a limitation in expressing love and worship to the Lord Jesus in your own native tongue. There seems to be a barrier there for each of us. But the use of speaking in tongues breaks the language barrier. It gives your spirit the vehicle with which it can express its love for the Lord.

A Methodist woman, who was baptized in the Spirit a while back, wrote to say she didn't know such rapture of worship was possible on this earth.

It's tremendous just to let our souls express themselves to the Lord in a language we can't understand, and this includes singing with the Spirit. Not only do we do this on our own, but as a company of people. It's wonderful when the Spirit leads us into worship, singing in tongues. The Holy Spirit just harmonizes everybody together; and since He is the Conductor, when He drops His baton, we all stop together. I have found this to be one of the most heavenly experiences. And the Lord gets all the benefit, when we all sing to Him in the Spirit.

Finally, I would like to share another wonderful expression of the use of speaking in tongues I have found in my own private devotions. There are times when we all fail and sin, which means we were "in the flesh."

Now we know that "if any man sin, we have an advocate with the Father, Jesus Christ the right-eous..." (1 John 2:1). And, "If we confess our sins, he is faithful and just to forgive us our sins, and to cleanse us from all unrighteousness" (1 John 1:9).

So I repent and believe the blood of Jesus cleanses me immediately. God, at that moment, forgets my sin and will never remember it against me again (see Hebrews

10:17).

But the devil will do everything in his power to make sure I don't forget it. He will tell me I've let the Lord down, I've let the church down. In fact, he'll tell me that I myself am "a let-down." But this is what I have discovered: He can't possibly condemn me while I'm in the Spirit. I sinned because I was in the flesh. So the secret is to get back into the Spirit and out of the flesh as soon as possible. And that is only a step of faith away. The bridge between the flesh and the Spirit is faith.

I believe that one step of faith is to speak with tongues and praise the Lord. The moment I do that it lifts my spirit above my flesh and puts me out of reach of the devil's condemnation. "There is therefore now no condemnation to them which are in Christ Jesus, who walk not after the flesh, but after the Spirit" (Romans 8:1).

This then I find to be a valuable use of speaking in tongues. Praying in tongues edifies me, builds me up, improves me, and helps me day by day to walk with Jesus in the other gifts and the fruit of the Spirit.

Part Two

PRODUCING CHARACTER

CHAPTER 14

A FRUITFUL TREE

Before any tree can grow and bear fruit a seed must be planted. The largest and most productive apple tree in any orchard was once a tiny seed, planted, cultivated and nourished until it grew to fruition.

So it is for all of us who are called to bear the fruit of the Holy Spirit in our lives. A seed is planted in our spirits when the Holy Spirit comes to reside in us, and the source of all our growth in the fruit begins at that point.

As we have said earlier, the fruit of the Spirit is the character of Jesus Christ, actually the very nature of God. In His earthly ministry, Jesus manifested an exceeding amount of the fruit of the Spirit, "love, joy (gladness), peace, patience (an even temper, forbearance), kindness, goodness (benevolence), faithfulness; (meekness, humility) gentleness, self-control (self-restraint)..." (Galatians 5:22,23 *The Amplified Bible*). These traits were evident in the way Jesus treated those around Him, from the woman caught in the act of adultery, to the young children that just wanted to get close to Him in the crowds.

And now that Jesus has gone to be with the Father, He has sent the Holy Spirit to impart the fruit of the Spirit to us, that we might develop the character of Jesus Christ. God, the Holy Spirit, possesses these same characteristics, the same nature as Jesus. Therefore, as the Holy Spirit lives in us, we have the seed of the fruit of the Spirit in our lives, and the potential to bear it abundantly to the blessing of all those around us.

This source from God is certainly the initial step in bearing fruit. But that seed must be cultivated, pruned and nourished so that it can grow into a fruitful tree in the Kingdom of God.

In the following chapters we will be looking at the characteristics of each of the fruit of the Spirit. And we will examine both the seed source and some vital nourishment for growth from the Word of God. One way we can definitely cultivate and nourish the fruit of the Spirit in our lives is to receive the encouragement and admonition of the apostles and prophets concerning the fruit. And we also have the precious and exciting promises of God to provide fertile soil for the cultivation and growth of the character of Jesus Christ in our lives.

CHAPTER 15

LOVE IN ACTION

Love Towards God

Love is something that is vital. God is speaking to His people about love these days in a very definite way; and we need to have clear teaching and understanding.

I believe we need to see the difference between just talking about love—and loving. This is the burden of the Lord's message—*loving*—getting down to the real thing. Not just having a doctrine of love, but the flow of love.

Jesus says, "If you love Me, keep My commandments" (John 14:15). In other words, "If you love Me, show that you love Me by the way you act." It is one thing to speak words. It is another thing to demonstrate action.

One of the first things you notice about two persons who love each other is that they try to please each other. They each try to give pleasure to the one they love. I wonder how many of us have given God pleasure by the way we have loved Him. The Lord Jesus set out to show us how much He loved the Father. In speaking of His Father, Jesus said, "For I do always those things that please him" (John 8:29). The Bible also tells us that Jesus didn't do one single thing unless He first got His instructions from the Father. Everything the Father asked Him to do, He did. And that is how we know that Jesus loved Him. He pleased the Father with His actions here on earth.

Now there are three areas in which the fruit of the Spirit, love, needs to be cultivated. Our love will be directed firstly towards God, secondly to one another, and thirdly to the lost.

The Bible is very specific in telling us how we should love the Lord. When questioned as to which is the most important commandment, Jesus answered, quoting from the Old Testament, "Hear, O Israel; the Lord our God is one Lord: And thou shalt love the Lord thy God with all thy heart, and with all thy soul, and with all thy mind, and with all thy strength . . ." (Mark 12:29,30).

This is the way to love God. Let us take this to heart. Do we love the Lord in this way? If we do, then we love Him as much as possible, because there is nothing else left. That weighs up the total being of man—the heart, soul, mind and strength. This is the way God wants us to love Him—with every part of our being.

Our heart

"Thou shalt love the Lord thy God with all thy heart . . ." The heart seems to be closely connected with loving. When two young people fall in love, they say that they love each other with all their hearts—the very center of their being.

You cannot live unless your heart is beating. If you have a fatal heart attack, they will write on your death certificate "heart failure" because the physical heart is vital to life—the central part. In the same way, spiritually speaking, God wants us to love Him with the very central part of our beings—wholeheartedly.

Our soul

"Thou shalt love the Lord thy God...with all thy soul." The soul consists, in part, of the *will* and *emotions*. Do you love the Lord with your *will*? This is where a lot of people find problems.

Self-willed, self-centered people are constantly having problems. We have to die out to those areas in our lives where we want our own way and will.

This is what Jesus did. He wasn't a softie. When he was praying in the garden of Gethsemane he cried out to the Father, "Not My will, but Thine be done." But first of all He said, "If it be possible, let this cup pass from Me." He said in effect, "I don't want to go to the cross if I don't have to, Father. But if it is Your will for Me, I love You with My will so much that I want Your will to be My will." Do you love the Lord like that?

Then, we must love the Lord with our *emotions*.

Let us ask ourselves the question, "Who made our emotions?" Did you? Did your father or mother? No. God made our emotions. He put them within us, and He put them there for a purpose. Not so we could go down to the local nightclub and have a wild time to fulfill them. I believe our emotions are to be fulfilled in God.

There are many who have problems in their emotional lives because they are afraid to let go and pour them out to the Lord.

That dear woman in Luke, chapter seven, who came to Jesus and broke the alabaster box and poured that precious ointment on His feet, and washed them with her tears, and wiped them with her hair. What was she doing? She was pouring her emotions out on the Lord Jesus Christ.

And what did the Lord say? "Her sins, which are many, are forgiven; for she loved much: but to whom little is forgiven, the same loveth little" (Luke 7:47).

I too love the Lord much because I have been forgiven much. That means I am willing to pour my emotions in love to the Savior, and He is worthy of all of it.

Some people have the idea that loving the Lord much, because one has been forgiven much, means that the worst of sinners, when they are saved, love the Lord the most. I don't agree with that. The smallest sin is big enough to send a person to hell, and what you may think was a small sin was enough to crucify the Son of God. Therefore, when people have a revelation of the immensity of sin, they realize the greatness of Christ's salvation. And they know they have been forgiven much. So they love much.

When you realize what Jesus did for you, you will love Him a lot. You will pour your emotions out upon Him.

Now I am not advocating emotionalism. I have no time for whipping up emotions artificially. When Elijah offered sacrifice on Mount Carmel, the Scriptures say that he put no fire under it. Instead, he called the fire down from heaven. And when we respond in faith to God, the heavenly fire comes down upon us and our emotions are poured out to Him in love.

What are some of the ways that we can pour out our emotions before God? The Bible makes them very clear.

We can sing to the Lord, clapping our hands and making a joyful noise, both with our mouths and with musical instruments: "Make a joyful noise unto the Lord, all the earth: make a loud noise, and rejoice, and sing praise.... With trumpets and sound of coronet make a loud noise before the Lord, the King" (Psalm 98:4,6); and "O clap your hands, all ye people; shout unto God with the voice of triumph" (Psalm 47:1). We can also show our emotions to God by dancing and leaping before Him just as King David did (2 Samuel 6:16), whom the Bible says was a man after God's own heart (Acts 13:22).

I believe there are times when God gets just as excited as we do. The Scriptures tell us that one day God laughed in the heavens. Hallelujah! Let us pour out our love upon Him. We are to love the Lord with all our heart and all our soul.

Our mind

Then, "love the Lord thy God... with all thy mind." We must love the Lord with our minds. How often we get problems in our thought life. No wonder Paul, writing to the Philippians, says, "Whatsoever things are true...honest...just...pure...lovely...of good report; if there be any virtue, and if there be any praise, think on these things" (Philippians 4:8).

Get your thinking capacity filled with the love of God. Oh, if God's love fills your mind, you'll find yourself thinking loving thoughts all the time.

We must also love the Lord with our "intellect" which refers to our capacity for understanding and acquiring knowledge. Loving the Lord with the intellect is something which is vital in these days when people are making so much out of education.

If you want to know what education is doing, just look around the world and you will find out. The intellect which has been educated without Christ is a dangerous thing. One of the worst things that some missionary societies have done is to go to the mission field and educate the natives without giving them Christ; hoping that somewhere along the line they would become religious.

This does more harm than good. Give the people Christ. *Then* give them education. I believe the mind that becomes intellectual and loves the Lord is great. But the mind that becomes intellectual and doesn't love the Lord is a very dangerous thing.

Whatever you have in intellectual ability, may I suggest that the best thing you can do with it is to use it for the glory of God.

Perhaps many years of study have been put in to bring you to the standard of education you have acquired. Bring your intellect to the place where it loves God and you will only want to use it for His glory.

Our strength

Finally, we are to love the Lord our God with all our strength, with all our capacity, more than anything or anyone else in the world. That is the definition of a true disciple.

Loving the Lord with all of our capacity is best illustrated in the scripture, "If any man come to me, and hate not his father, and mother, and wife, and children, and brethren, and sisters, yea, and his own life also, he cannot be my disciple" (Luke 14:26).

I had a lot of trouble with that verse when I

discovered it as I was studying about becoming the Lord's disciple. "If you don't hate the closest ones in your family you cannot be My disciple," is what Jesus is saying.

I asked, "Lord, what does it mean?" I searched out the Greek word and found that it was even stronger. It really did mean hate. I sought the Lord on this, and then it came home very clearly what it meant.

It means that our love for the Lord is so great that our love for wife, children, and other fellow members of the family *looks* like hate in comparison. It does not mean, of course, that we actually hate them. It means that we love them very much, but that we love God much more.

We see a picture of this kind of love when Jesus died on the cross. Do you believe God loved His Son the Lord Jesus? On the cross Jesus cried out, "My God, My God, Why hast Thou forsaken Me?" Do you really think at that moment it looked as though God loved His Son? It looked as if He hated Him. But I believe the heart of the Father God in heaven was deeply hurt. The love that the Father in heaven had for His Son upon the cross was as great at that moment as it had ever been. But it didn't *look* like it. God *so* loved the world, that He gave His Son to die that cruel death.

I had an experience a few years ago when it looked as if I didn't care about my family. When our little daughter Faith was born, she was a late arrival, and I was soon due to leave for Japan. She arrived only a few days before I had to go and it was very heartbreaking. But Heather and I prayed about it and I went as scheduled.

When I returned, a young woman came up to me and said, "Reverend Double, I want to apologize to you."

"Oh," I said, "how's that?"

"Well," she replied, "I've been criticizing you. When you left your wife a few days after your baby was born and went all the way to Japan for a month, I criticized you because I felt it could never be right, God wouldn't want you to do that."

I turned to her and replied, "If you only knew what it cost me! But it was Heather who wanted me to go more than I wanted to go myself, because she knew it was the will of God, and that God had called me to do it."

I believe God is speaking to us all about this kind of commitment. In the next chapter we are going to look at our love for one another, and there is a great emphasis on this at the moment within the Body of Christ. But we need to beware, because if the devil cannot hold us back, he will go to the other extreme and push us too far. I believe the balance comes through when we put our love for God first.

We need to be careful that we are not loving one another so much that we are forgetting to love our God. And remember, our love for God is not just words, it is a commitment to obey Him come what may.

Let us have that kind of commitment to the Lord, and love Him with all of our hearts, our souls, our minds, and with all of our strength.

Cultivating the Fruit of Love

Loving God

God's seed of love
The Bible says that we can love God *"because he first loved us"* (1 John 4:19). The depths of His love toward us is often overwhelming, and the greatest example of that love is contained in the well-known passage, *"For God so loved the world,* that he gave his only begotten Son, that whosoever believeth in him should not perish, but have everlasting life"* (John 3:16). Other scriptural examples of God's love toward us are:

"Herein is love, not that we loved God, but that *he loved us,* and sent his Son to be the propitiation for our sins" (1 John 4:10).

"But *God commendeth his love toward us,* in that, while we were yet sinners, Christ died for us" (Romans 5:8).

Paul states that nothing "shall be able to separate us from *the love of God,* which is in Christ Jesus our Lord" (Romans 8:39).

Paul also prays that we would all come "to know *the love of Christ,* which passeth knowledge, that (we) might be filled with all the fulness of God" (Ephesians 3:19).

Jesus spoke to the disciples of the greatness of His own love in a foreshadowing of His death when He said, *"Greater love hath no man than this,* that a man lay down his life for his friends" (John 15:13). That is definitely the kind of love that Jesus demonstrated on Calvary.

The Apostle John also declares, "Behold, *what manner of love the Father hath bestowed upon us,* that we should be called the sons of God" (1 John 3:1). John goes on to reveal that *"love is from God"* which reminds us that God's love is only planted in our hearts by the power of the Holy Spirit (Romans 5:5) and that we can allow our love for God to grow and produce abundant fruit in our lives.

Our rewards for loving God
There are some marvelous and specific promises that God has given to those who truly love Him.

God living in us: Jesus said that if we love Him and would abide in Him and His words, that both He and the Father would come and make their abode in us (John 14:23).

All things working for good: The Bible says, "And we know that all things work together for good to them that love God, to them who are the called according to his purpose" (Romans 8:28).

Riches beyond our imaginations: "Eye hath not seen, nor ear heard, neither have entered into the heart of man, the things which God hath prepared for them that love him" (1 Corinthians 2:9).

The promise of grace: "Grace be with all them that love our Lord Jesus Christ in sincerity" (Ephesians 6:24).

The promise of a crown: "He shall receive the crown of life, which the Lord hath promised to them that love him" (James 1:12).

CHAPTER 16

LOVE IN ACTION

Love Towards Man

Loving one another

To link our loving God to our loving of one another, we turn to 1 John 4:20,21; "If someone says, 'I love God,' and hates his brother, he is a liar; for the one who does not love his brother whom he has seen, cannot love God whom he has not seen. And this commandment we have from Him, that the one who loves God should love his brother also" (*NASB*).

We can see that there is a definite link between loving God and loving our brothers. There are some people who are completely unbalanced in this matter. They'll say, "Oh, yes, I love the Lord. But I just cannot get along with Sister Gray, so I sit on the other side of the church on Sundays. And I go out of the other door so that I won't have to meet her."

You cannot love God Whom you cannot see, if you don't love your brother or your sister whom you can see. You are only being hypocritical if you think you can.

John 13:34,35 says, "A new commandment I give to you, that you love one another, even as I have loved you, that you also love one another. By this all men will know that you are My disciples, if you have love for one another" (*NASB*).

Please note that it doesn't say that we'll be known as a disciple of Christ if we preach about love, pray about love, sing about love, or hold it as one of our dearest doctrines. No, it says very clearly that we are only His disciples if we *have* love one for another.

I believe there are some couples in our congregations who don't have this love for one another. The husband wouldn't lay down his life for his wife, and the wife wouldn't lay down her life for her husband.

If you are a young person and hoping to marry, make sure you don't marry a person for whom you would not be willing to die. Examine your love and ask yourself the question, "Is my love that kind of love? Is it something that I would suffer for if need be?"

When you stand before the minister and make your marriage vows, you promise to love your partner for better, for worse; in sickness and in health. I believe that is saying that you are willing to lay down your life for the other.

You are not marrying the other person for what you can get out of them. You are marrying them because you are willing to give your life for them. This is the kind of love that sticks and that works today. And this is the kind of love that the members of the Body of Christ are supposed to have for one another.

Love is a commitment. It has a respect, a trust within it. It is not good enough just having it as a doctrine or having it preached at us. I believe that commitment and submission to one another calls for two persons within the Body of Christ to love each other with a divine love placed there by the Holy Spirit (Romans 5:5).

This kind of commitment and love toward one another was exemplified in the Old Testament by the relationship between David and Jonathan, King Saul's son. Jonathan made a covenant between their households because "he loved him (David) as he loved his own life" (1 Samuel 20:17 *NASB*). And when Saul attempted to have David murdered out of jealousy, Jonathan's commitment of love remained. He said to David, "The Lord will be between me and you, and between my descendants and your descendants forever" (1 Samuel 20:42 *NASB*). Jonathan was willing to lay down his life for David: the kind of love which Jesus Himself says is the best, "Greater love hath no man than this, that a man lay down his life for his friends" (John 15:13).

I can be committed to someone whom I know loves me. When they love me there's no problem. I know God loves me, therefore I can trust Him with my life. I can trust Him for all my needed provision. I can trust Him for my family, for my possessions, and for my journeyings.

It is the same in being committed and submitted to one another because I can trust those I'm committed to. If I know somebody loves me, I can throw my life down and say, "I'm committed to you, brother, sister." And I know that they'll be faithful and loyal in love.

God is calling the Body of Christ to this kind of loving today. We need each other. We cannot do without each other.

There are some brothers to whom I am committed that I very rarely see—sometimes only once or twice a year. But when we do meet and greet each other with a holy hug, it is somehow like a long, lost loved one coming home, because we are a part of each other.

The Body of Christ is not just a bunch of individuals wandering around doing their own thing. The members of Christ are members of a body, and should be committed and submitted to each other in loving one another.

It is a good thing to realize that love is not sympathy. In fact, I believe that mere sympathy can easily become sin. Sympathy says, "Oh dear, I am sorry to hear that, Mrs. Brown. Well, see you again next week." That has no relation to the love of God whatsoever.

To love another brother or sister means that we have compassion. Now there is a big difference between compassion and sympathy. Compassion is the love of God reaching out to do something.

Compassion says, "Sister Brown, I am sorry, and I want to help you. Can we pray about it together? Can I do something? Can I go down the street and shop for you?" Compassion moves in to the situation and acts.

Jesus in His ministry was moved with compassion. He got involved in the needs of mankind. He got involved in the needs of people in their homes.

He saw a woman coming down the street following a coffin in which lay her only son. She was a widow and had no one else to support her. There was no welfare state, so she couldn't go to the social security bureau and collect any benefits. Jesus put out His hand and said, "Stop. Open up the coffin." Then He raised that dead son to life again. That is love and compassion. He did something about it.

Ask yourself the question, "Do I have any compassion for the person next door to me. Would I get involved with him?" This is loving one another as Christ loved us, laying down one's life for others.

First John 3:17-19 tells us, "But whoever has the world's goods, and beholds his brother in need and closes his heart against him, how does the love of God abide in him? Little children, let us not love with word or with tongue, but in deed and truth. We shall know by this that we are of the truth, and shall assure our hearts before Him" (*NASB*). Isn't that beautiful?

If we have this world's goods, something in our possession, whether it is faith in God to work a miracle in that persons's life, whether it is a wordly possession, finances, help of any sort; if we withhold it and just say, "Oh, I love you," and close our hearts and shut out our compassion, the Bible says we are not of the truth.

We must love in deed and in truth. The word truth means reality. God's love is real. Hallelujah! I tell you wherever the love of God is you feel it. If I go into a home to stay and the love of God is there, I can feel it before I have been in the door many seconds.

Loving is giving. We always quote Luke 6:38, "Give, and it shall be given unto you..." as relating to finances, but that is only one aspect of it. This is a picture of love. Love keeps giving. I believe we should live to give, and as we give, we also receive.

How about people who are feeling lonely? There is no need to feel lonely. Just start loving people. Start giving of your love and what will you find? Others will be loving you in return.

One of the saddest things is to see people who don't seem to be able to receive love. I put my arms around someone, and it is like putting my arms around a tree for all the response there is. They shut themselves up, put up their shield of self-defense. They just cannot receive affection.

I have seen people who, having been ministered to and counseled, have begun to break as they have felt the love of God. Sometimes all a person needs is someone to put his arms around him and give him a good holy hug, and to feel the love of God flowing from that person. It has broken through the rebellion and resentment, the bitterness and the problems in his or her life.

The Bible says concerning the Gospel, "... how shall they hear without a preacher?" (Romans 10:14). We could paraphrase that and say, "How shall they feel love, without a lover?" You are not just meant to be someone who knows the Scriptures rather well. God needs you so that He can love other people through you. He has no hands but your hands. He has no feet but your feet. Let the love of God flow out. Start to give in this way.

But some Christians are bound by fear. They say, "Oh, if I start loving people like that, what will happen? How can I start exposing myself in that way?"

It's true that when you start loving someone you begin to expose yourself, to open yourself up. But, "There is no fear in love; but perfect love casteth out fear..." (1 John 4:18). Let God's love fill your heart. Let God's love flow out through other people and the fears will go.

When you love one another it's a wonderful feeling. There are some people I could expose my heart to. I could really let them know every secret in my heart because they love me, and I love them. There is no fear between us. And I know that if I did something vitally and seriously wrong, there are some people to whom I could go and share it with them. I know that the first thing they would do is forgive me and set about putting me right. That is the kind of friend I like. We all need this kind of friend in the Body of Christ.

Loving your enemy

Another aspect of loving others is given to us in Matthew 5:44: "Love your enemies." What a tremendous thing! One of the reasons why we have enemies is so that we can love them!

Now as far as I know, I don't have any enemies, but there are people who set themselves up as my enemies. They are there. Always putting a monkey wrench in the works. Always causing something to happen. If they can destroy you they will. Maybe not by actions, but by words. But we are to love our enemies. Love them to death. Destroy their animosity with love. In other words, you love them so much that you want them to be your friends, and they just can't hold out and be your enemy any longer.

Many years ago as a young Christian, I walked into my house and walked into a scene where I could easily have committed murder. Instead, at that moment, God filled my heart with His grace and love, and I walked over to the man who had wronged me and put my arms around him and kissed him.

My action didn't appear to do anything in the situation at that moment. It certainly didn't change the circumstances. But in recent years, God has shown me that by loving my enemy I was saved from bitterness and resentment, and from many problems that could have occurred in my life, had I not allowed the love of God to flow through me.

It is important to love your enemies because of what it is going to do for you. It's going to keep you free, and in the love of God. It will protect you from many problems and sometimes from sickness, because there are many illnesses which are caused by resentments and bitterness that people harbor inside them. Above everything else, it will keep you right with God.

Paul, writing to the Romans in chapter 12 verse 19-21, explains the same thing to them, "Never take your own revenge, beloved, but leave room for the wrath of God, for it is written, 'Vengeance is Mine, I will repay, says the Lord. But if your enemy is hungry, feed him, and if he is thirsty, give him drink; for in so doing you will heap burning coals upon his head.' Do not be overcome by evil, but overcome evil with good" (*NASB*).

To put it another way, in the Sermon on the Mount, Jesus said, "Bless them that curse you." So another way of loving your enemies is to bless them.

If you find that someone has set himself up as an enemy against you, don't start fighting back and saying, "I'll show him!" Get down on your knees and pray for him instead. And this is the way to pray for that type of person, "Lord, please bless him, as You have blessed me." This allows the Lord to minister to your enemy as He sees fit. That is the way to love your enemy.

Loving those who hurt you

There are some who have been hurt by others. God knows all about these hurts. People have been cruel and unkind, but even so, for your own sake—love them. "Love never fails." Love will keep the blessing of God upon your life.

Proverbs 10:12 says, "Love covereth all sins." Love doesn't go around exposing other people's sin. Love doesn't hang other people's dirty washing on the line. Love covereth.

If you see a brother overtaken in a fault, what do you do? Do you get on the telephone and tell the pastor? No. You go down to that one, and in a spirit of meekness, you restore him (Galatians 6:1). That is love.

One of the worst things I hear is when wives come to me criticizing and pulling their husbands to pieces, telling me about how bad and weak they are, what failures. That makes me feel sick inside. If you love your husband or vice versa, you cover them. Every one of you should say that you have the best wife, or husband in the world. I believe that is important.

Loving the lost

Finally, we read in 2 Corinthians 5:14-15, "For the love of Christ constraineth us; because we thus judge, that if one died for all, then were all dead: And that he died for all, that they which live should not henceforth live unto themselves, but unto him which died for them, and rose again."

Hallelujah! The love of God constrains us to love those for whom Christ died—the lost and dying people of this world.

One of the things which concerns me in the Body of Christ is the lack of concern for reaching out to the multitude who are on their way to hell and a lost eternity. We need to keep balanced. Let us not get lopsided. Let us love God, love one another, love our families, and let us also love the lost who are out there in a dying world.

I say this with all my heart, if our love doesn't go over the wall, as it were, outside the camp, then it has been a failure. If the love which God has poured upon us doesn't go back home to our neighbors and friends, to the people with whom we work, and to our relatives, to reach them for Jesus, then we have failed. I have often said, "If I cannot win souls to Christ, I would rather die and go straight to heaven." And I mean it.

The night I was converted to Christ, when I was introduced to the Lord Jesus by His servant, Vic Ramsey, I was thrilled. I tingled all over. I was forgiven! I felt I'd had a spring cleaning inside. Oh, it felt good. And I have discovered that every time I lead a soul to Jesus Christ, I get that same thrill.

Oh, hallelujah! There were tears streaming down my face when I received Jesus, and they often stream as I see souls come to Christ and accept Him as their Savior, too.

When I stand before thousands in Dar Es Salaam, Tanzania, as I have done on several occasions, preaching the Gospel to them, and see Moslems, in tears, falling to the earth as they bow to accept Jesus as their Savior; I tell you I feel the thrill I felt on the night I was saved.

Oh, the preciousness of a human soul, so great that God gave His only Son to die for them. God gave everything He had for lost humanity, which included you and me. And since He did that for me, I don't feel I can give less for those in the world around me.

We must go and tell them that God loves them. We need a John 3:16 love ourselves. Our love must be expressed in sharing the Lord Jesus Christ with the world—not a doctrine, not a denomination, not a formality or a book of rules, but a Person, the Lord Jesus.

I believe the whole world is looking for what I have. They may not be able to name it. They may not realize what they are looking for, but all are basically trying to find satisfaction and purpose in life. They are all seeking after something which we who know Jesus have. Let us give it to them in the love of God.

How do we do it? Nothing tells us more clearly than that wonderful love chapter in the Word of God, 1 Corinthians, chapter 13. We quote from a paraphrase by a missionary to India. It is called, "Love that grips the heart." Ask yourself whether you fit in here or not.

If I have language ever so perfect and speak like a great teacher, and have not the knack of love that grips the heart, I am nothing. If I have decorations and diplomas and am proficient in up-to-date methods, and have not the touch of an understanding love, I am nothing....

If I have all faith and great ideals and magnificent plans and wonderful visions, and not the love that sweats and bleeds, and weeps and prays and pleads, I am nothing.

If I surrender all prospects, and leaving home and friends and comforts give myself to the self-evident sacrifice of a missionary career, and turn sour and selfish amid the daily annoyances and personal slights of a missionary life; and though I give my body to be consumed in the heat and sweat and mildew of India, or some other mission field; if I have not the love that yields its rights, its coveted leisure, and its pet plans, I am nothing, nothing, nothing. Virtue has ceased to come out of me.

If I can heal all manner of sicknesses and diseases, but wound hearts and hurt feelings for want of love that is kind, I am nothing.

If I can write books and publish aritcles that set the world aglow, and fail to transcribe the word of the cross in the language of love, I am nothing, nothing, nothing.

The greatest words of love that were ever spoken on this earth, were spoken by the Son of God, the Lord Jesus Christ, on the cross, "Father, forgive them; for they know not what they do" (Luke 23:34).

Similar words were taken up by a human being just like you and me, who was feeling just the same kind of hurt and pain—Stephen the martyr.

As those boulders were hurled against his body, God opened the heavens and Stephen saw Jesus. As he saw Him, he cried out, "Lord, lay not this sin to their charge" (Acts 7:60). In other words, "Father, forgive them."

Romans 5:5 tells us, "The love of God is shed abroad in our hearts by the Holy Ghost which is given unto us." This is the only way we can love people, by giving the Holy Spirit His way in our lives.

As we do our part in yielding our whole selves to Him, so He will bring forth the choice fruit of love in abundant measure.

Cultivating the Fruit of Love

Loving the Brethren

Love's vital source
It is God's love exhibited to man through the Old and New Testament that gives us our perfect example of how we are to love one another. But the Lord not only gave us the demonstration of His love, He also gave us the means to acquire it.

Remember, the Bible says, *"The love of God is shed abroad in our hearts by the Holy Ghost which is given unto us"* (Romans 5:5). We are assured that the fruit of love can grow in our hearts and become part of our character because God has planted the seed of that love in our hearts by the power of the Holy Spirit. The rest is up to us as we follow the biblical encouragement and admonition to love.

Encouragement to love
Some words of nourishment in cultivating the fruit of love are:

"Seeing ye have purified your soul in obeying the truth through the Spirit unto unfeigned love of the brethren, see that *ye love one another with a pure heart fervently"* (1 Peter 1:22).

"For this is the message that ye heard from the beginning, that *we should love one another*" (1 John 3:11).

"Owe no man any thing, but *to love one another*" (Romans 13:8).

As we learn to love one another, we find that love truly permeates every area of walking in the Kingdom of God. It is not just words that are limited to friendly church services, but a way of walking through our Christian experience and growing up into the fullness of Jesus Christ. The Bible admonishes us that we are not to merely love in word or tongue, but as Jesus did, we are to love *"in deed and truth"* (1 John 3:18).

We are also admonished that *"faith worketh by love"* (Galatians 5:6); *"by love serve one another"* (Galatians 5:13); we are to *"forbear one another in love"* (Ephesians 4:2); *"speak the truth in love"* (Ephesians 4:15); *"provoke one another to love"* (Hebrews 10:24). And we should also, *"walk in love," "love in faith and sincerity,"* and be *"knit together in love."* Love is truly an all-encompassing fruit of the Spirit in our Christian lives!

Benefits for loving the brethren
Many promises have been given to those who keep the Lord's commandments. Jesus said that if we keep His commandments *we shall abide in His*

love (John 15:10). The Apostle John has said that if we keep the Lord's commandments that *He dwells in us and we in him* (1 John 3:24). Abiding in Christ's love and dwelling in Him can be ours if we obey this commandment from Jesus, "This is my commandment, *That ye love one another,* as I have loved you" (John 15:12).

We are perfected in love: The Bible says that "If we love one another, God dwelleth in us, and his love is perfected in us" (1 John 4:12).

We are able to bless others: "For we have great joy and consolation in thy love..."(Philemon 7).

We'll be known as disciples: "By this shall all men know that ye are my disciples, if ye have love one to another" (John 13:35).

We'll know of our eternal life: "We know that we have passed from death unto life, because we love the brethren" (1 John 3:14).

We'll know we are of the truth: "My little children, let us not love in word, neither in tongue; but in deed and in truth. And hereby we know that we are of the truth..." (1 John 3:18, 19).

We'll know we are born of God and know Him: "Beloved, let us love one another: for love is of God; and every one that loveth is born of God, and knoweth God" (1 John 4:7,8).

CHAPTER 17

JOY IN THE LORD

Joy is one of the top grade commodities that God would put in His shop window to advertise the Christian life.

If you know anything about business, you know that a man shows the best he has to offer. He doesn't use anything in his window that looks a bit tatty. He makes his display really beautiful.

For this reason, I believe joy is a very important part of Christian life. It is one of the things God uses to attract others and advertise salvation. There is nothing this world has to offer that can possibly compare with the joy of the Lord.

The Bible says, "The joy of the Lord is your strength." You show me a Christian who has no joy, and I'll show you a weak Christian. You show me a Christian who is full of joy, and I'll show you a strong Christian. In other words, there is strength in joy.

If you look through the life story of Jesus, you will find that whenever He saw the disciples discouraged, downhearted, having problems, full of fear, or about to go under, one of the first things He did was to tell them to get some joy into their lives.

One night the disciples were out in the midst of the Sea of Galilee, when suddenly a storm blew up and they began to be in fear and dread. All they could see was the strong possibility of a watery grave.

Jesus appeared walking on the sea and said, in effect, "Cheer up. Don't be downhearted. Get some joy back into your lives."

You will find that Jesus uses these words many times in the Gospels. God wants to bring cheer into people's lives. How can we ever hope to convey the message of salvation to others, unless we have some joy to share with them as well?

One day, a man stood in the street handing out tracts. Dressed in black and clutching a black umbrella, he looked very somber as he stood on the corner.

"Want one?" he asked gloomily as a prospect approached him.

"What is it?" the passer-by asked suspiciously.

"A Gospel tract," answered the melancholy Christian. The stranger took the tract and read the title *Abundant Life.*

"No, thanks," he replied curtly. "If that's it, I don't want it."

A true story! But there are a lot of people going around advertising the Kingdom of God who are giving that kind of impression. No wonder no one is interested. Yet the Christian life in reality is the most thrilling and adventurous life there is. Hallelujah!

Now I think we need to realize that joy is something altogether different from happiness.

You could go to an exciting Christian conference,

and because of the environment you could be happy. Then by the time you were back at work again on Monday morning those feelings could all have evaporated. Happiness depends upon happenings and is related to the environment you are in.

The Bible speaks of people being able to enjoy the pleasures of sin for a season. Don't go around telling people they can never be happy in the world, because, sad to say, some of them seem to be a lot happier than some Christians do! Before I was saved, I used to be happy sometimes. But it depended on my environment.

You see, if someone has $50,000 to spend, he is happy. The prodigal son was very happy while he had it all. He had friends and lived riotously. He really got a kick out of life. But he only had this transitory thing called happiness. When the money was gone, so was the happiness, and he ended up with the pigs in the pigsty.

Joy is different. Joy has no relationship to environment. Joy depends on Jesus. And He is the same yesterday, today and forever.

Monday morning in the factory, or back at home, Jesus will be just the same as He was at the conference or in the church.

Psalm 16 tells us that in His presence there is fullness of joy, and at His right hand there are pleasures forevermore. Though we may not always realize it, we live in His presence. We cannot get out of His presence even if we try, because He is everywhere.

Now if we begin to live in the consciousness of His presence by faith, and relate to Him in everything that happens, we find that joy is there all the time.

The news will change. Things will probably get worse, as the Bible warns, but Jesus never changes. If the price of gasoline continues to go up, it makes no difference to me. The currency of heaven isn't about to be devalued. God is still going to supply all my needs, however much it is. We don't live in relation to our circumstances. We live in relation to Him!

A certain brother, Ken Tahoven, flew into Nairobi during the Mau Mau uprising when Christians were being martyred because of their refusal to enter into the evil covenant. One of the Kenyan Christians met him and asked, "How are you, Mr. Tahoven?" "Oh, I'm feeling a little bit travel sick, and tired, having traveled from South Africa," he replied.

The Kenyan Christian answered, "I didn't ask you how you were physically. How are you spiritually?" Ken Tahoven said it shook him up, and he set out to investigate what was behind this man's outlook.

He discovered that this young man, a pastor, had already suffered much for his faith in God. Like most people in Kenya, he owned a small plot of land, a few animals (which are local currency in lieu of money) and lived in a simple mud hut with his wife and children.

One Sunday, the Mau Mau watched and saw him go off into the bush to preach. When evening came and his wife and children were alone in the hut, they wired up the doors and windows and set fire to it. Then they slew every one of his chickens and sheep and cattle, and hid in the bush to see what he would do.

When he returned and saw that his family had been burned to death, and his animals all slaughtered, he knelt down in the ashes, lifted up his hands to heaven and prayed Job's prayer, "The Lord gave, and the Lord hath taken away. Blessed be the name of the Lord."

The Mau Mau hiding in the bush were so bowled

over by this expression of the Kingdom of God in this man, that they turned and ran for their lives. The joy of the Lord was his strength. His environment, serious as it was, couldn't tell him anything. Instead, he immediately related to his God. What a standard!

If we are living in relation to things around us, they will tell us all sorts of lies, and what they are really saying is that God is going to fail us. Circumstances try to tell us that He is about to let us down because something has happened, or because there is what appears to be bad news. "Oh," we panic, "everything is about to go wrong." Of course it's not. God is in control. God is able.

God has exalted Him (Jesus) far above all, and we are in Him. Complete in Him. Our joy comes to us constantly from our relationship with the Lord Jesus Christ.

It's amazing how many people get bothered about the weather. The first day I arrived at a certain town for a conference it was raining and blowing and cold. Someone said, "Not a very nice first day here. Not a very nice welcome for you is it?"

I said, "It's wonderful." I will not allow this negative stuff to affect me. It *is* wonderful. The weather doesn't make the slightest difference. Jesus doesn't change. But the weather is going to change. Yes, it is going to rain and snow, and get frosty. That is a foregone conclusion. It happens every year. But why should this affect us? Why should we feel good or bad according to whether the sun is shining or not? The sun is shining in my heart all day and every day. It doesn't even go in at night time.

I know a man in Scotland who gets up in the

morning, pulls back the curtains and looks out. If it's foggy (they get a lot of mist in Scotland), he stretches his hands to heaven and says, "Thank You, Lord, for a wonderful, foggy morning." He is living in joy. He goes through to victory, and the day becomes a wonderful day.

Relationships with others also seem to affect some people in much the same way that the weather does. A man will say, "It's all right for you, Reverend Double, but if you had a wife like mine. . . ." Well, I don't have his wife. But I do *have* one. Then they say, "If you had my children." Sure, I don't have their children. But I do have five of my own!

Some even say, "If you had to work for my boss," or, "If you had a foreman like I have, you would never be able to live the Christian life and have joy all the time. He is full of filth—swearing and cursing with every word."

Yes, but I have had a boss. And I have had that type of foreman or manager, too. I used to be a salesman. On Saturdays we had to wash and clean our vehicles, and mid-morning we would have a cup of tea or coffee with all the workers of the factory where the product was made. There would be about two hundred there.

This foreman was the foulest-mouthed, swearing, cursing man I think I have ever met. Yet when they came asking me to buy raffle tickets, and I said, "No thank you, I'm a Christian," and all the fellows and girls began to laugh and mock, calling me Moses and Holy Joe, this man spoke up. He said, "Don't you dare mock Don Double. He has got the guts to stand up for what he believes. You leave him alone."

Yes, the world knows when it sees the real thing, and

will honor it. Many times God will stand up on our behalf if we let our joy in Him be expressed, so that our environment is not telling us anything.

There in the factory where you work. There in the home with your wife, your husband, your children. There with all the problems of life. There is where you should be expressing your joy.

I believe it is impossible to go under if we are relating properly to the Lord, because my Bible tells me that no man takes this joy from us (John 16:22). No one can make us lose our joy. When we are relating to Jesus through it all, we find that the joy of the Lord is our strength, even at the crisis hour.

It is no use saying it is your wife who takes away your joy, or because you were up all night with the children and didn't get any sleep, you haven't any joy.

I have often said to my wife, Heather, when our children have been teething and kept us awake at night, "Now is the time to praise the Lord." It is! If you are praising the Lord you are relating to God straight away.

The Bible says, "With joy shall you draw water out of the wells of salvation" (Isaiah 12:3). Joy is the bucket with which you get the water out of the wells. When you begin to praise the Lord in adverse circumstances, you are letting down the bucket so that you get some water. In those wells of salvation is everything you will ever need for body, soul or spirit. Joy has tremendous healing virtue, too. It is like medicine.

I make it a practice when I get up in the morning to say to the first person I meet, "It's the greatest day you ever lived." I don't find out their circumstances first, or ask how they are feeling.

When Tony Mettrick, who plays the organ in our

crusades, joined us, I used to greet him in the mornings like this. "Tony, it's the greatest day you ever lived." Tony would rub his eyes and say, "Some of us are slower starters than others."

I didn't take any notice of that, but the next morning it would be the same. "Tony, it's the greatest day you ever lived." But Tony was a really slow starter. It was about 11 or 12 o'clock before you could get any joy out of him.

However, it was not long before Tony was out looking for me first. "Don, it's the greatest day *you* ever lived." He is a completely changed man! At our camps he is the first one up, and he shouts it over the loud speakers, "It's the greatest day you ever lived." Then he follows it up with a music tape:

This is the day, this is the day
That the Lord hath made, that the Lord hath made.
We will rejoice, we will rejoice
And be glad in it, and be glad in it . . .(Psalm 118:24).

He is full of joy, and before the rest of us are up, he will have been down to town and bought the newspapers. It has changed him. The joy of the Lord is a permanent thing. And all you have to do is relate to the Lord in every circumstance, and live in this tremendous joy.

The Bible tells of "Joy unspeakable, and full of glory." There are times when one can be speechless with the joy of the Lord. I know I can make a lot of noise

126

at times, and not all of us are the same. But you can still have joy, even if it is the unspeakable sort. It will show on your face.

Eyes tell an awful lot. You can look into a person's eyes, and if there is joy there his eyes will be sparkling, his face shining, and that smile will be relating to you.

Today we have automation and machines, and you can only know what is going on in the machine by what registers on the dial. It is the same with us human beings—you can know what is going on inside by what registers on the dial.

Joy makes such a difference. You should have seen us one night in the tent at the Blaithwaite camp. About 10 o'clock I gave the benediction, and we were all intending to go to bed. Suddenly something hit the tent. I know it was the Lord. I can't explain it because it was entirely unexpected.

The whole congregation exploded and everyone began to praise God and worship the Lord. It went on for about two hours, and people who had never danced in their lives before were dancing before the Lord. I have never known anything so infectious.

Across the way in the prayer tent, several were being counseled, and the counselors were finding it hard going. But about the same time that something hit our tent, something hit their tent, too. All the hardness went. People began to weep and repent. Then the weeping turned to joy, and they returned to the main tent to rejoice with the rest of us. There were people there that night who have never been the same since, because the joy of the Lord had been expressed.

It is a wonderful thing to dance before the Lord. We

so often think that dancing belongs down in the ballroom with the latest band leader and his orchestra. I tell you, long before any of them were born, David was dancing before the Lord with all his might (2 Samuel 6:14).

Also, way back in Israel's history, a mighty deliverance took place when the whole nation was delivered from the bondage of Egypt. The first thing that happened after Moses and the children of Israel reached the other side of the Red Sea was that Miriam took out her tambourine and began to play and dance before the Lord, expressing their joy.

Joy is very positive. You can't have negative joy. It doesn't exist. The Bible speaks of being "nourished up in the words of faith." Some of those words of faith are words of joy and faith.

I meet someone and he says, "How are you?" I answer, "I'm excellent." That is about the best word I can find.

How are you? I've heard people say, "You must be careful how you answer because you must be honest."

Now what is honesty? I believe honesty is truth. What is truth? Jesus said, "I am the way, *the truth,* and the life: no man cometh unto the Father, but by me" (John 14:6). In other words, *He* is the truth. *He* is reality. Not me! Not my environment. Not my feelings or my circumstances. He is the truth, so I am confessing how He is, and how He is, is how I am. The Bible says so; "... as He is, so are we in this world" (1 John 4:17).

I don't think He has a headache or depression! He's not feeling downcast or defeated. He is fine, and as He is, so am I. And when I begin to confess how He is, that truth, that reality, becomes my experience also.

Joy is a fruit of the Holy Spirit. A fruit which our lives can bear in abundant measure if we learn to relate by faith to Jesus at all times, and in all circumstances.

Cultivating the Fruit of Joy

Our source of joyful life
In developing the joyful character of the Master,
Jesus Christ, we can look to the Father and the Son
for our source and example.

The Lord possesses the character of joy, "The
Lord thy God in the midst of thee is mighty; he
will save, *he will rejoice over thee with joy*; he will
rest in his love, *he will joy over thee with singing*"
(Zephaniah 3:17); and *"He brought forth His
people with joy,* His chosen ones *with a joyful
shout"* (Psalm 105:43 *NASB*).

Jesus has given us His Word to instill His joy
within us. "These things have I spoken unto you,
that *my joy might remain in you,* and that your
joy might be full" (John 15:11).

We also obtain our joy in the Lord by simply
being in His presence, as David declared in the
Psalms, "In thy presence is *fulness of joy;* and at
thy right hand there are *pleasures for evermore"*
(Psalm 16:11). Jesus Himself spoke of the joy of
His presence with His disciples, "I will see you
again, and *your heart shall rejoice,* and your joy
no man taketh from you" (John 16:22).

Ways to have joy in the Lord
The joy of the Lord is like a bubbling brook of everlasting water. As we let it flow out from our hearts, we continue to bear the fruit of joy in our lives.

"Be glad in the Lord, and *rejoice*, ye righteous: and *shout for joy*, all ye that are upright in heart" (Psalm 32:11).

"Shout joyfully to the Lord, all the earth. *Serve* the Lord *with gladness;* Come before Him with *joyful singing"* (Psalm 100:1,2 *NASB*).

"Let the godly ones *exalt in glory;* Let them *sing for joy* on their beds" (Psalm 149:5 *NASB*).

"Let all those who put their trust in thee *rejoice:* let them ever *shout for joy*...let them also that love thy name *be joyful in thee"* (Psalm 5:11).

"My soul shall be *joyful in the Lord*: it shall *rejoice in his salvation"* (Psalm 35:9).

"Rejoice in the Lord always: and again I say, *Rejoice!"* (Philippians 4:4).

Benefits of joy
We have strength: "The joy of the Lord is your strength" (Nehemiah 8:10).

We can defeat our enemies: When three large armies came against King Jehoshaphat of Judah, he sent out the singers before his own army, to rejoice before the Lord saying, "Praise the Lord; for his mercy endureth for ever." And when they began to sing and praise, the Lord set ambushments against their enemies and they were defeated (2 Chronicles 20:21, 22). We can defeat our enemies of depression, worry, or adverse circumstances in the same way by praising the Lord.

Our sorrow and mourning shall flee away: "Therefore the redeemed of the Lord shall return, and come with singing unto Zion; and everlasting joy shall be upon their head: they shall obtain gladness and joy; and sorrow and mourning shall flee away" (Isaiah 51:11). Jesus came to give us "the oil of joy for mourning, the garment of praise for the spirit of heaviness" (Isaiah 61:3).

We can draw nourishment from the Lord: "Therefore with joy shall ye draw water out of the wells of salvation" (Isaiah 12:3).

We can encourage and uplift one another: "Speaking to one another in psalms and hymns and spiritual songs, singing and making melody with your heart to the Lord" (Ephesians 5:19 *NASB*).

CHAPTER 18

PEACE

Peace is another precious fruit of the Spirit. How marvelous it is when one meets people who are, what I call, ministers of peace. Jesus said, "Blessed are the peacemakers: for they shall be called the children of God" (Matthew 5:9).

There are not many peacemakers around. Not even in church. When I talk of peacemakers, I mean those who carry something special with them. Wherever they go they seem to breathe the peace of God. They walk into fiery situations, and the moment they move in they minister peace. The very environment changes because the peace of God is there.

Now I am not talking about your individual peace *with* God. You have peace *with* God when you are saved. The moment you get right with God and your sins are forgiven, you have peace with God.

But I am talking about the peace *of* God, and that is far different. God wants us all to have this peace.

What is peace? Have you ever stopped to think? Well, first of all, peace means the war is over! You can't have peace and be at war. Many people's hearts, including those of some Christians, are like a battlefield.

The Bible speaks of the flesh warring against the Spirit and the Spirit against the flesh. But it also tells us, "Ye are not in the flesh, but in the Spirit, if so be that the Spirit of God dwell in you. Now if a man have not the Spirit of Christ, he is none of his" (Romans 8:9).

Do you have the Spirit of Christ? Does the Spirit of God dwell in you? Then you are not in the flesh. You are in the Spirit. Start believeing it, and peace will come. Hallelujah! The war is over. You know this glorious peace and you can begin to minister it out to others.

We find too that this is the peace that passeth all understanding. I can't explain it to you. It is impossible. If the Bible says it is past understanding then it is. It is peace that can exist in the midst of the worst possible circumstances.

The Bible says, "Be careful for nothing (stop worrying, fretting and being anxious); but in every-thing by prayer and supplication with thanksgiving let your requests be made known unto God. And the peace of God, which passeth all understanding, shall keep your hearts and minds through Christ Jesus" (Philip-pians 4:6, 7).

Worry is a sin. Anxiety and fretting are sins because they are unbelief. It means a lack of confidence in God. It means you don't really believe that He has everything under control, that He sits and rules and reigns as the Sovereign of the universe, that He knows all about even you.

I chuckle sometimes when I hear people say, "Lord, You know everything about me." Of course He does.

134

When you reach this wonderful state where you know that God knows, then you can have peace.

Fear is another thing that troubles many people. Big problems come to people's lives and families because of fear.

Now we all find our confidence in God in different ways. For that reason, I don't like to hear somebody who has found his confidence in God in one scripturally sound way, trying to knock the foundation from others who have found their confidence in God in another way; leaving them without one, trying to make everyone conform.

For example, some people these days are preaching against faith in the blood of Christ for protection. Now, some believe there is tremendous protection in "claiming the blood" and others apparently do not.

A man came down to our church, where some had tremendous faith in the blood of Christ for protection, and preached against it. That night these people who had previously been tremendously peaceful people, powerful people, without a fear in the world, found their ground of peace shattered. Someone had to walk home with some of them in the dark because this brother had taken away their confidence. We had to personally counsel them, reminding them of the scriptural foundation for faith in the power of the blood of Christ. Once their faith was restored, the fears were removed.

It doesn't matter how you find your biblical confidence in God as long as you find it. And when you have confidence in God, you have the peace of God. You know He is in complete control.

Personally, I am a great believer in the blood of

Christ. I believe it spelled the devil's defeat for time and eternity. I believe God is Sovereign and He is in charge. There is nothing that can catch God off guard. He never slumbers or sleeps. Twenty-four hours a day He is tenderly watching over us. Isn't that wonderful?

You don't have to do anything other than trust Him. You can bring everything to Him in prayer. Whatever comes against you, you can commit it to the Lord. You can put it in His hands, and He will take good care of it.

He will work it all out, and what is more, when He works it out it will be for your good. "And we know that all things work together for good to them that love God, to them who are the called according to his purpose" (Romans 8:28).

Think again of the occasion when Jesus stepped into a boat with His disciples and said, "Let us go over unto the other side." The Bible says they launched forth. The Lord, having given the word that they were going over to the other side of the lake, put a pillow in the corner of the boat, lay down and went to sleep. He was confident that His Father in heaven had heard the word He had spoken, and as far as Jesus was concerned, it was as if He were already there. He had spoken the creative word of faith, and His Father would see He arrived safely.

Halfway across, a storm arose. The wind began to howl and the disciples heard it. Their sense of hearing was giving them information, and they began to be concerned.

At the same time, they saw with their eyes how the waves beat against the boat, rocking it perilously. Water was beginning to get in. Another sense was giving them information.

Then you can be sure that as the wind and waves were

beating against the ship, they were feeling it on their faces. Their clothes were wet and they were probably standing in a bit of water. Their sense of touch was now feeding them information.

Several of their senses were telling them they were in trouble, and they were all upset and anxious.

But there was *Peace* asleep on a pillow. It didn't bother Him a bit. He just slept on through it all. Finally, the disciples came along and shook Him, "Wake up, Jesus, don't You care that we perish?"

Jesus might have answered, "Have you forgotten that I said we were going over to the other side?" The Reverend Oral Roberts once said that they could not go under for going over, because Jesus had given His word. Peace can sleep on a pillow in the midst of a storm.

Jesus in this world was just a carpenter. Those fishermen in the boat with Him had been out in all sorts of weather. They were used to the sea. They knew all the tricks of the trade. Yet they were scared and talking about perishing.

How about us? Are we going to be like the disciples and say, "Lord, don't You care that we perish?" Or are we going to allow His peace to come and rule and reign in our lives?

The moment the disciples called on Jesus, He stood up in the boat and demonstrated peace. He rebuked the wind and waves, and there was a great calm. The storm was over because Jesus Himself is Peace.

"Peace" in the Greek refers to security in the turmoil. We certainly get some turmoil in this world, but we are in the hands of Jesus. Nothing that goes on around us can shake us from His hands.

He holds us tightly, and He has promised that He

will never let us go. Let us believe it for therein lies our peace.

God gives His peace to us continually, as we learn to rest in Him in every situation.

Cultivating the Fruit of Peace

The Lord has supplied many ways for us to obtain peace, but all of them have their beginning in Him for *"The Lord will bless His people with peace"* (Psalm 29:11).

How we acquire our peace
If we love the Word of God: "Those who love thy law have great peace" (Psalm 119:165 *NASB*).

If we think on the Lord: "Thou wilt keep him in perfect peace, whose mind is stayed on thee: because he trusteth in thee" (Isaiah 26:3).

If we are righteous before God: "And the work of righteousness shall be peace" (Isaiah 32:17).

If we obey the Lord's commandments: "There is no peace for the wicked" (Isaiah 48:22 *NASB*); but if we obey the commandments of the Lord our peace will be like a river (Isaiah 48:18).

If we follow after Jesus: He assures us, "Peace I leave with you, my peace I give unto you: not as the world giveth, give I unto you" (John 14:27).

If we listen to the words of Christ: "These things I have spoken unto you, that in me ye might have peace. In the world ye shall have tribulation: but be of good cheer; I have overcome the world" (John 16:33).

If we pursue after peace: "So then let us pursue the things which make for peace" (Romans 14:19 *NASB*).

Walking in peace

Many times in the New Testament we have been called to walk in peace, often by the Lord Jesus Himself, as He said in Mark 9:50, "*... have peace one with another.*"

The Apostle Paul, following the Lord's leading, exhorted many of the churches to "*be at peace among yourselves*" (1 Thessalonians 5:13). Paul declared that "*God hath called us to peace*" (1 Corinthians 7:15) and that together we are to "endeavor to keep the unity of the Spirit in *the bond of peace*" (Ephesians 4:3).

To the church at Rome Paul admonished, "If it be possible, as much as lieth in you, *live peaceably with all men*" (Romans 12:18). And finally, the writer of Hebrews exhorts the brethren to "*follow peace with all men*" (Hebrews 12:14).

The benefits of peace

As there are rewards and benefits to growing in

each of the fruit of the Spirit, the following are some of the rewards for cultivating and nourishing the fruit of peace in our lives.

We have guidance from God: "Let the peace of God rule (umpire) in your hearts" (Colossians 3:15).

We have joy: "...counselors of peace have joy" (Proverbs 12:20 *NASB*).

We have a posterity: "For the man of peace will have a posterity" (Psalm 37:37 *NASB*).

We are called children of God: Blessed are the peacemakers: for they shall be called the children of God" (Matthew 5:9).

We will sow the fruit of righteousness: "And the seed whose fruit is righteousness is sown in peace by those who make peace" (James 3:18 *NASB*).

God is with us: "...live in peace; and the God of love and peace shall be with you" (2 Corinthians 13:11).

CHAPTER 19

PATIENCE

Do you ever get your patience ruffled? There is plenty of opportunity for the manifestation of patience (or longsuffering) in our roles as parents, and in our relationships with one another at every level.

One of the ways we can know the fruit of the Spirit, patience, in our lives is in the small spiritual skirmishes that happen day by day.

The Bible says it is the little foxes that spoil the vines, and certainly it is the little things that trip the believer who is moving into maturity, more than the big things for which he is already alert.

One day I was washing my car down with a bucket of water and a sponge. I was doing fine and had nearly finished, when suddenly the bottom of my trouser leg caught in the bucket and tipped it over my shoe, sock and trousers. "Praise the Lord," I responded cheerfully, and went inside to change. As I thought about it later, it became a great blessing to me, for I found the Lord showing me the work of grace He had done in my life, and the patience He had given me. A few years previously, I would have gone in, thrown my shoe, sock and trousers across the room and said, "Look what happens when I try to do anything."

Again the Bible says do all things without murmurings and disputings. When the boss comes along and wants you to do some insignificant job, how do you react? Do you think, "That isn't right. This is not my job. There are about ten other persons who joined the firm after me. I have seniority; I'm being mistreated." Or do you manifest the fruit of the Spirit, patience, and do the job gladly?

We also need to realize that it is trials and testings of this nature that actually work patience in us.

It plainly says in Romans 5:3 that tribulation is what works patience into our characters. Therefore, to acquire more paitence we need tribulation, testing, trials.

The Bible also tells us that all those who live godly in Christ Jesus *will* suffer persecution (2 Timothy 3:12). But while we are suffering, our patience has the opportunity to grow.

We often find ourselves being persecuted in some way because of our faith, and there is the temptation to fight back. It is at that moment that we need to know the manifestation of the fruit of patience.

Paul's thorn in the flesh illustrates this apsect of patience very well. Many Bible commentators declare that Paul's thorn was not physical sickness, and I wholeheartedly agree with them, because of the context.

Second Corinthians 12:7 tells us that the thorn in the flesh was a messenger of Satan sent to buffet Paul.

Paul had received an abundance of revelation from God, and the purpose of the thorn was that he should

143

not be puffed up with pride and exalted above measure.

Verse 10 tells us that Paul took pleasure, that is patience or longsuffering, in weaknesses, insults, distresses, persecutions, and in difficulties for Christ's sake (*NASB*).

He declared, as will all those who know the fruit of patience, "When I am weak, then am I strong."

Second Corinthians 11: 24-27 describes, I believe, Paul's thorn. It is a list of his sufferings, mainly through persecution.

Paul prayed three times that this messenger of Satan would be taken away, and he was told by God that His grace was sufficient for him.

This grace was the grace of patience. In 2 Corinthians 12:9 Paul speaks of his weaknesses (*NASB*). And if our bodies had been through the list of persecutions Paul mentions in chapter 11, I'm sure we would be weak, too. Notice, Paul speaks of being weak, not of being sick.

Wherever God sent Paul, there were two things Paul could be sure about. One, he would experience a mighty anointing upon his ministry. Two, the persecutors would be there, waiting with their whips, their rods and their stones. This is what Paul prayed would be taken away. But he found grace in his persecution, and manifested patience.

While persecution is taking place, it is obviously very unpleasant. Yet when it is over, we can see that it has quietly produced the fruit of patience in our characters.

It is important to accept persecution in the right spirit, because those who fight back, and who try to justify themselves, never have any manifestation of this fruit of the Spirit.

There is a tremendous word in Psalm 119:71. "It is good for me that I have been afflicted; that I might learn thy statutes." The affliction of persecution teaches us things we would never learn any other way.

"It is good for me that I have been afflicted...." This affliction, I believe, is never sickness, because the cross of Christ dealt with sickness; and by exercising our faith in Christ's finished work at Calvary, we can receive healing.

"Who his own self bare our sins in his own body on the tree...by whose stripes ye were healed" (1 Peter 2:24); "...that it might be fulfilled which was spoken by Esaias the prophet, saying, Himself took our infirmities, and bare our sicknesses" (Matthew 8:17).

I know there are those who have found a deeper relationship with God when they have been sick, but I believe it is always God's purpose to bring us through to health.

When we think of patience, we must not look upon it as a negative virtue. We are not merely to endure, but to take pleasure in afflictions as Paul learned to do, and praise the Lord as He takes us through.

The secret of learning to praise when everything seems to be going against us is the victory into which the Lord wants to bring us all.

Afflictions may come, and persecutions may come, but it is always God's will for us to triumph in Christ, no matter what the situation. "But thanks be to God, who always leads us in His triumph in Christ, and manifests through us the sweet aroma of the knowledge of Him in every place" (2 Corinthians 2:14 *NASB*).

The word "triumph" in the Greek means to have great success; and through the manifestation of the fruit of patience, I believe we can come through to this place of victory in our Christian lives.

Cultivating the Fruit of Patience

Patience is a virtue that will endear us to many of the people around us. God exemplified His patience to the wayward children of Israel and Christ revealed His patient character with His questioning apostles. We can also learn to develop and grow in this same fruit. And by it we can reveal a part of Christ's character to our husbands and wives, children and friends, our bosses and our fellow employees. Allowing the Lord to develop patience in our lives will bring the maturity of Jesus Christ.

Christ's patient example
Because of his persecution of Christians before he met Jesus, the apostle Paul felt that in Christ's forgiveness he had experienced the real depth of patience, "And yet for this reason I found mercy, in order that in me as the foremost, Jesus Christ might demonstrate *His perfect patience,* as an example for those who would believe in Him for eternal life" (1 Timothy 1:16 *NASB*).

Realizing Christ's endless patience, Paul questioned the Roman church, "...do you think lightly of the riches of *His* kindness and forbearance and *patience*?" (Romans 2:4 *NASB*). Later, he goes on to encourage them, "Now the *God of patience* and consolation grant you to be like-minded..." (Romans 15:5).

We also know from Peter, who sorely tested the Lord's patience at times, that *"The Lord* is not slow about His promise...but *is patient toward you,* not wishing for any to perish but for all to come to repentance" (2 Peter 3:9 *NASB*).

How we acquire patience

There are several ways that we can acquire patience. Paul exhorted the church at Colossae to "put it on"; "And so, as those who have been chosen of God, holy and beloved, *put on a heart of...patience"* (Colossians 3:12 *NASB*). Paul also prayed that the Colossians would attain *"patience...with joyfulness"* (Colossians 1:11); and he admonished Timothy to flee the lusts of the flesh and instead to *pursue* "righteousness, godliness...*patience...*" (1 Timothy 6:11 *NASB*).

But often, the most complete way to attain patience is through the trials and testing that come into our lives. Paul reassures us, "But we glory in tribulations also; knowing that *tribulation worketh patience"* (Romans 5:3). Patience is such an important characteristic of our Christian walk that we can have joy in our trials because we know we will attain it.

The apostle James echoes Paul's words, "Consider it wholly joyful, my brethren, whenever you are enveloped in or encounter trials of any sort.... Be assured and understand that *the trial and proving of your faith bring out* endurance...and *patience*" (James 1:2,3 *The Amplified Bible*).

How we move in patience

As servants of the Lord we are to walk *"in much patience"* (2 Corinthians 6:4). And in all things that we do, whether preaching the word, or exhorting and encouraging the brethren, we are to do it *"with great patience* and instruction" (2 Timothy 4:2 *NASB*).

We are to have *"patience of hope* in our Lord Jesus Christ" (1 Thessalonians 1:3); while the older men in Christ are exhorted to be *"sound...in patience"* and the "older women likewise" (Titus 2:2,3).

The apostles encourage us, "We exhort you, brethren... *be patient toward all men"* (1 Thessalonians 5:14). And "... let us *run with patience* the race that is set before us, looking unto Jesus the author and finisher of our faith" (Hebrews 12:1,2).

Finally, Paul reminds us that we are to "... *walk* in a manner worthy of the calling with which you have been called...*with patience*" (Ephesians 4:1,2 *NASB*).

How our patience is rewarded
We will inherit the promises of God: "...be not slothful, but followers of them who through faith and patience inherit the promises" (Hebrews 6:12). "...after he (Abraham) had patiently endured, he obtained the promise" (Hebrews 6:15). "For ye have need of patience, that, after ye have done the will of God, ye might receive the promise" (Hebrews 10:36).

We will bring forth fruit: In the parable of the sower and the seed, Jesus spoke of the good ground, which are the believers who "having heard the word, keep it, and bring forth fruit with patience" (Luke 8:15).

We will be perfect (mature): "...let patience have her perfect work, that ye may be perfect (mature) and entire, wanting nothing" (James 1:4).

CHAPTER 20

KINDNESS

Kindness is a very precious fruit of the Spirit. You don't find that many people refuse kindness. In fact, there are people all around the world looking for others who will be kind to them.

One of the problems I find in my own ministry and experience is that because of my size (6 feet, 5 1/2 inches) I tower above most people and have to look down at them. Consequently, I am very conscious of my need for the fruit of kindness in my life, lest people I am ministering to should feel I am pressuring them or forcing them into something. I thank God He has enabled me to know a degree of this kindness when handling people in my ministry.

When counseling someone, there may be things in that person's life that stick out very obviously as major problems, and anyone with a bit of spiritual perception can recognize them immediately.

The temptation then is to go right in and bash away at the problems, but in doing so you may destroy the one you are trying to help, or cause him to rebel.

This is where kindness comes in. As you lead that seeker gently to the Lord, relying on the Holy Spirit to guide, you find that before long he is recognizing the problem without you even telling him.

Kindness is a wonderful fruit of the Spirit, and of great importance in the counseling ministry—one which all counselors would do well to cultivate.

It is very easy to be hard, strict and legal. Many of the problems around us today are caused by strict legalism. Legalism produces a veneer of righteousness that men hope others can't see through. They want to appear holy, but are only fooling themselves.

In place of this legalism, we need to know the kindness that our Lord gives which has with it the stamp of authority from heaven.

The Bible says, "And be ye *kind* one to another, *tender-hearted*, forgiving one another, even as God for Christ's sake hath forgiven you" (Ephesians 4:32). We need to be this tenderhearted in our lives and ministries.

Many of the Lord's people could do with showing tenderness to their own families, the wife to the husband, the husband to the wife; parents to children, children to parents.

A person who shows kindness and tenderheartedness to someone outside his family but cannot show it to the people in his own home, is not right with God.

These are days in which the world needs to see genuine kindness. But it needs to be displayed in our family life first, and is one of the visible evidences to the world of true Christian character.

To be sensitive is also very, very important. Many people are hurt by the insensitivity of other Christians, and I believe we really need to pray that God will make us tenderhearted, kind, and give us sensitivity, so that we can feel the other person's position. Then when we minister, or even have just a conversation or discussion, we will not hurt the other but be sensitive to his needs.

Jesus can still be touched with the feeling of our infirmities, and we need to be touched in a sensitive, tenderhearted way towards others.

Tenderness and kindness take time. They are never in a hurry. Very often we hurt others by rushing instead of taking time with them. Kindness cannot live in an atmosphere of clock watching.

Take the perfect example of the life of our wonderful Lord Jesus Christ. There has never been a man before or since with such a kind, tenderhearted ministry.

We see Him taking time to be tender with the small children crowding around Him, saying, "Suffer the little children to come unto me and forbid them not for of such is the kingdom of heaven."

How often we tend to forbid people or loved ones to take time with us, when it is so necessary that we show them kindness.

The Lord Jesus took time to go eighteen miles out of His way to the well at Samaria, to meet that one woman who was in such great need and living immorally. He took time to minister to her, and she went with the message of His love burning in her heart back to her own city. As a result, many people came running out to see this wonderful Person.

He also had time for the woman taken in the very act of adultery, who had lost her dignity and her pride, and was in a sorry state. It is so heartwarming to see how kind He was with her. After He had dealt with the religionists who were condemning her, He brought her to the place of forgiveness, and sent her on her way with the authoritative word, "Go, and sin no more."

In Jesus' example, it is easy to see that many of the fruit of the Spirit are interwoven. In this case, the fruit of kindness is born out of the fruit of love. When speaking to the questioning crowds about love of our neighbor, Jesus used a simple story of how to show that love by an act of kindness.

A certain man was going down from Jerusalem to Jericho; and he fell among robbers, and they stripped him and beat him, and went off leaving him half dead.

And by chance a certain priest was going down on that road, and when he saw him, he passed by on the other side.

And likewise a Levite also, when he came to the place and saw him, passed by on the other side.

But a certain Samaritan, who was on a journey, came upon him; and when he saw him, he felt compassion,

and came to him, and bandaged up his wounds, pouring oil and wine on them; and he put him on his own beast, and brought him to an inn, and took care of him.

And on the next day he took out two denarii and gave them to the innkeeper and said, "Take care of him; and whatever you spend, when I return, I will repay you" (Luke 10:30-35 *NASB*).

That was an act of kindness that can serve as an example to us all.

There is much hardness in the world today. I am

convinced that one of the most effective ways of reaching people with the Good News of the Gospel is through kindness.

Everyone in the world is looking for real love. They may not realize it, but when it comes they will recognize it. Many people are wounded and heartbroken inside. To bring them a Savior Who is kind, and Whose desire is to heal them body, soul and spirit by His tender touch, would release many of them from the knots all tied up inside them and from irrational fears that grip their lives.

This world, which is so frustrated and floundering, needs to know that the Lord Jesus is kind, that He cares and loves and is the answer to every need there is in life today.

Cultivating the Fruit of Kindness

Heaven's kind source
As with all the fruit of the Spirit, the source and example of kindness is God, Who has blessed us with *"the riches of His kindness"* (Romans 2:4 *NASB*).

In the Old Testament, Nehemiah speaks of divine kindness, "But thou art *a God...of great kindness*" (Nehemiah 9:17). And the Lord spoke of Himself through Isaiah, "For the mountains shall depart, and the hills be removed; but *my kindness shall not depart from thee...*" (Isaiah 54:10).

Paul forthrightly declared to Titus that the kindness of God resulted in our salvation, "But when *the kindess of God our Savior...* appeared, He saved us" (Titus 3:4,5 *NASB*). Surely this is kindness beyond measure!

Encouragement for kindness
Solomon, in all his God-given wisdom, declared that *"What is desirable in a man is his kindness"* (Proverbs 19:22 *NASB*). It is also quite desirable for a woman, for when Solomon speaks of the "excellent wife" in Proverbs 31, one of her many virtues is that *"the teaching of kindness is on her tongue"* (Proverbs 31:26 *NASB*). Blessed be the

man *or* woman who has a word of kindness in their mouth!

Paul had some definite things to say about the fruit of kindness. He encourages all the saints to *"...be ye kind one to another,* tender-hearted, forgiving one another, even as God for Christ's sake hath forgiven you" (Ephesians 4:32); and he exhorts the church of Rome to *"Be kindly affectioned* one to another with brotherly love..." (Romans 12:10).

Paul continues by asking the Colossians to *"Put on* therefore, as the elect of God, holy and beloved, bowels of mercies, *kindness..."* (Colossians 3:12).

Benefits of our kindness
If we are kind:

We will have the Father's approval: James admonished us "to visit orphans and widows in their distress." This act of kindness is important enough to be considered "pure and undefiled religion in the sight of our God and Father" (James 1:27 *NASB*).

We will keep our reward: Jesus promised, "Whoever...gives to one of these little ones (humble folk) even a cup of cold water to drink, truly I say to you he shall not lose his reward" (Matthew 10:42 *NASB*).

We will inherit the Kingdom: If we display these acts of kindness; giving food to those who hunger, drink to the thirsty, clothes to the naked, hospitality to strangers (and friends alike); if we visit the sick and the imprisoned, we are assured a reward—the inheritance of the Kingdom (Matthew 25:35,36). For the King, Jesus, has promised to welcome us, "Come, you who are blessed of My Father, inherit the kingdom prepared for you from the foundation of the world" (Matthew 25:34 *NASB*).

CHAPTER 21

GOODNESS

Goodness is at the heart of God. God is totally good. And from Him goodness proceeds in a continual flow.

Now, when the world looks at a Christian, one of the things it expects to see more than anything else is goodness. Yes, and the world has a right to expect it, for if God's Spirit dwells in us, there should be an outflow of goodness from us as well.

One of the meanings of goodness is excellence. Excellence is second-mile Christianity.

I was talking to a school teacher recently. After examinations at the end of the school term, she writes on each student's report card, "poor," "fair," "good," "very good," or "excellent." She explained to me that "excellent" means that the student has done more in the examination than was actually necessary.

This, of course, is what I mean by second-mile Christianity. The first mile is expected of you. It is what you need to do. Without it you don't even qualify to be recognized as a normal Christian.

But the second mile is voluntary. It takes you beyond

obligation—far more than you need to do. This is excellence. This is the life of goodness. Doing the over and above out of the delight of your heart. Manifesting the life of the Lord Jesus within you.

I recall an instance during a crusade when a certain woman allowed a team member to use her automatic washing machine. The team member put the wash in the machine and then went off to do some necessary shopping, returning two hours later to find the clothes not only washed, but dried and ironed as well.

Of course, it was a spiritual thing to allow the use of the washing machine in the first place. The Bible teaches us to share what we have—to have all things common. But to take the clothes and actually iron them; that was going the second mile.

Goodness also means generosity. Goodness gives and gives, and gives again, whether it be money, time, or life itself.

Christianity is not just concerned with spiritual experiences. The Christian life has to be lived right here on earth and should be wonderfully practical.

Another meaning of goodness is virtue, in the sense of being a force or a power. Goodness is certainly a great force in the world as we witness and share the Gospel of the Lord Jesus Christ with the community in which we live.

Virtue can also mean reliability, trustworthiness. I believe it is very important that Christians today should be reliable, able to be trusted to produce what is expected.

Goodness expresses the very nature of God and can only be manifested when self is crucified and Christ is at the center of our being.

Most of the great men and women who make their mark in life are those who have learned the secret of self-sacrifice, and have been set free from self-centerdness. They give their lives for others and seek to make a contribution to the advancement of life.

A group of young people just finishing their education and preparing to make decisions about the future were asked what they wanted to do with their lives and why.

Each, without exception, showed a completely selfish motive for deciding his future occupation, decisions being based on how much money he could make or how much attention he would receive.

Later, the group was asked to give the names of personalities from history who had been really great and had made an impact upon the scene of life. They all listed men and women who had given self-sacrificing service to the world.

This shows that these young people recognized that true greatness stems from goodness and self-sacrifice. Yet they were not themselves prepared to follow such a path or to be of service to their fellow men. They only sought to gratify themselves.

This is typical of the day and age in which we live. But as Christians we should desire to be different. One of the greatest messages I ever heard preached was a sermon entitled, "Christians are different." And the only way we will be different is if we allow the fruit of the Spirit to be manifested through our lives, especially the fruit of goodness.

The Bible tells us that whatsoever a man sows he will reap. If you don't like what you are reaping, you must change what you are sowing. One cannot plant potatoes and hope to reap peas.

So it is in the Christian life. If you want to reap goodness, you need to make sure you are sowing goodness. If you want to reap a harvest from the realm of the Spirit, then you must make sure you are sowing the things of the Spirit.

Needless to say, goodness doesn't improve with education. It has nothing to do with intellectual ability. Yet many people base their morality on the pronouncements of the intellectuals of this world.

Philosophers become guides for society. We tend to feel that those with higher education and intellectual ability are more qualified than others to rule on moral issues. This is a totally wrong concept. Only God, the Source of all goodness and wisdom, has these answers.

The educators say—learn again. The philosophers say—think again. The religionists say—try again. But Jesus says—"Be born again" (John 3:3).

To be born again is to be born of God's Spirit, for that which is born of the Spirit is Spirit, just as that which is born of the flesh is flesh.

All true goodness comes from God's Spirit, and the person who has been born again has the very life of God within him and the potential to become all that God wants him to be.

Cultivating the Fruit of Goodness

The source of all goodness

"O taste and see that *the Lord is good:* blessed is the man that trusteth in Him" (Psalm 34:8). The Lord is truly good, and it is in His goodness that we find the source for this fruit of the Spirit, and the example to bear more of it. In the Psalms David cries, "The earth is full of *the goodness of the Lord*" (Psalm 33:5). And we who have been born into the Kingdom of God can echo that joyful call.

"The *goodness of God* endureth continually" (Psalm 52:1). Because God's goodness endures, we can use His example as nourishment in cultivating the fruit of goodness in our lives. We can believe that the Lord will continually help us to grow in goodness because He possesses it in Himself.

Encouragement for goodness

—"*Do good* to them which hate you" (Luke 6:27).

—"As we have therefore opportunity, let us *do good unto all men*" (Galatians 6:10).

—"And do not neglect *doing good* and sharing" (Hebrews 13:16 *NASB*).

—"Abhor that which is evil; *cleave to that which is good*" (Romans 12:9).

—"Ever *follow that which is good,* both among yourselves, and to all men" (1 Thessalonians 5:15).

—We are to be a people *"zealous for good deeds"* (Titus 2:14 *NASB*).

—"...So that you may walk in a manner worthy of the Lord, to please Him in all respects, *bearing fruit in every good work"* (Colossians 1:10 *NASB*).

—"Let your light so shine before men, that they may see your *good works,* and glorify your Father which is in heaven" (Matthew 5:16).

Benefits of goodness
The rewards of goodness are plentiful, as Jesus promised, *"...do good,* and lend, hoping for nothing again; and *your reward shall be great"* (Luke 6:35).

We reap goodness: "Do good, O Lord, unto those that be good" (Psalm 125:4); and we receive goodness, if we "continue in his goodness" (Romans 11:22).

We obtain favor: "A good man obtaineth favor of

the Lord" (Proverbs 12:2); and "He that diligently seeketh good procureth favor" (Proverbs 11:27).

We leave an inheritance: "A good man leaveth an inheritance to his children's children" (Proverbs 13:22).

We are satisfied: "The backslider in heart will have his fill of his own ways, But a good man will be satisfied with his" (Proverbs 14:14 *NASB*).

We receive praise from authority: "Do you want to have no fear of authority? Do what is good, and you will have praise from the same . . ." (Romans 13:3 *NASB*).

We have glory, honor, peace: "There will be tribulation and distress for every soul of man who does evil . . . but glory and honor and peace to every man who does good" (Romans 2:9,10 *NASB*).

We have wisdom, knowledge, joy: "For God giveth to a man that is good in his sight, wisdom, and knowledge, and joy" (Ecclesiastes 2:26).

We have eternal life: "Depart from evil, and do good; and dwell for evermore" (Psalm 37:27).

CHAPTER 22

FAITHFULNESS

The seventh fruit of the Spirit—faithfulness—means good faith, fidelity. A faithful person is one who is trustworthy.

God is faithful. He is trustworthy. That is why we are able to rely on Him and to have faith in Him. But can He trust *us*? Are *we* faithful?

We have already touched on this subject of trustworthiness under the fruit of goodness, for, as we said earlier, the fruit of the Spirit in certain aspects overlap. But Christians should be reliable. It should be possible to trust the word of a Christian and know that he will carry out what he has said.

There are Christians who glibly make promises and do not keep them. They think they mean what they are saying at the time, but lacking the fruit of faithfulness, they forget, or can't be bothered to fulfill their promises.

There are individual Christians and even whole churches who have promised to pray for certain missionaries, and to support them. Yet there are instances where that promise has been the last communication the missionary has received from the parties concerned.

One missionary mother received a letter from a woman she had never met, requesting the measurements of her children and herself, so that this person could make some new things for them before furlough.

The measurements were sent with grateful thoughts and praise to God for such wonderful provision. But this person was not faithful. That was the last the missionary family heard about the matter.

How about faithfulness in the return of borrowed property? Borrowed books? Borrowed money? It is said that at a large Christian convention some years ago, after a message along this line, the small local post office sold right out of money orders. Christians were busy paying off their debts and other commitments.

Faithfulness also includes things like punctuality; cleaning up after oneself; answering necessary correspondence within a reasonable space of time.

The fruit of faithfulness doesn't undertake responsibilities and then fail to carry them out. Faithfulness does the job properly, not half-heartedly. Faithfulness doesn't let people down.

A preacher traveled a long distance to speak at a certain church, and found that the pastor had forgotten even to arrange the meeting!

Of course we are all fallible, and there will be slip-ups and failures. But much could be avoided if we would major on cultivating the beautiful fruit of faithfulness.

Luke 16:10 tells us, "He that is faithful in that which

is least is faithful also in much." If we don't learn to be faithful in the little things, God will never be able to trust us with greater things.

Faithfulness is the one outstanding virtue praised by Jesus in the parable of the talents. "Well done, good and faithful servant; thou hast been faithful over a few things, I will make thee ruler over many things: enter into the joy of thy Lord" (Matthew 25:23).

Peter tells us in 1 Peter 4:10 to be "good stewards of the manifold grace of God." And Paul reminds us in 1 Corinthians 4:2, "Moreover it is required in stewards, that a man be found faithful."

We must be faithful in the use of the gifts God has given us; faithful in the sharing of our substance; faithful in the proclaiming of the Gospel of our Lord Jesus Christ.

Lastly, faithfulness means loyalty. Are you loyal to the Lord? Are you loyal to your family? Are you loyal to your wife, husband, your boss? Are you loyal to your church?

Remember, the fruit of faithfulness will not necessarily leave a dead church in order to go to a live one. Rather it will first seek to take the life of the Lord to the dead church and share it with them. Of course, if they don't want the life you bring and throw you out, then that's a different matter. But the fruit of faithfulness will produce loyalty, for better or for worse.

Proverbs 28:20 informs us, "A faithful man shall abound with blessings." Have you been conscious of a lack of blessing upon your life over a period of time? If so, it may be that you need to submit to the Lord and allow Him to prune off the old dead works of unreliability, moodiness and carelessness.

Start producing a crop of the fruit of faithfulness, and you'll discover a whole new dimension of blessing in your Christian life.

Cultivating the Fruit of Faithfulness

Faithfulness is a vital fruit of the Spirit in developing the character of Christ. In Jesus Christ we can see the perfect example of faithfulness both to *us* and to *His Father*, for He went to the cross and died that *God's plan* for redemption might be completed and *we* might have eternal Life.

God's faithfulness to us

David, the Psalmist, cried in love to the Lord, "Thy loving kindness, O Lord, extends to the heavens, *Thy faithfulness reaches to the skies*" (Psalm 36:5 *NASB*); and "With my mouth will I make known *thy faithfulness* to all generations" (Psalm 89:1). God Himself declares, "I will not...deal falsely in *My faithfulness*" (Psalm 89:33 *NASB*).

Moses and Jeremiah are two more men of God that proclaimed this message of God's faithfulness. Moses admonishes, "Know therefore that the Lord your God, He is God, *the faithful God*, who keeps His covenant and His loving kindness to a thousandth generation..." (Deuteronomy 7:9 *NASB*); while Jeremiah crys to the Lord, "*Great is thy faithfulness*" (Lamentations 3:23).

And we can be confident that God will fulfill all of

the promises recorded in the Bible, because we know that *"He who promised is faithful"* (Hebrews 10:23 *NASB*).

The rewards of our faithfulness

The rewards of faithfulness reveal the great importance of this fruit of the Spirit. Most often the faithful person is made a leader or steward of some of God's most precious gifts.

The Father of faith is Abraham, and because he was faithful before God, the Lord *established a momentous covenant* with him, granting Abraham the promise of an inheritance of land, and descendants more numerous than the stars in the sky (Hebrews 11:8-12).

In the rebuilding of Jerusalem after the destruction by the Babylonians, Nehemiah placed a man *in authority over the entire city* because he was "a faithful man" (Nehemiah 7:2); and Nehemiah chose several other men to be *treasurers over all the treasuries of the city* "for they were counted faithful..." (Nehemiah 13:13).

Paul declares that it is the faithful man who will be made *steward "of the mysteries of God"* (1 Corinthians 4:1,2). Anyone found unfaithful could not be trusted with such precious truth.

Paul goes on to admonish Timothy that God will

strengthen those He considers faithful, *putting them into service for Jesus Christ* (1 Timothy 1:12 *NASB*). In a later letter, Paul cautions Timothy to *entrust the truths of the gospel* to "faithful men" (2 Timothy 2:2 *NASB*).

When Jesus was speaking to the crowds that followed Him, He explained this spiritual principle of *receiving authority for faithfulness* by the parable of the talents. When the man with the five talents came back to his master with five more talents, the master said to him, "Well done, *thou good and faithful servant:* thou has been faithful over a few things, *I will make thee ruler over many things:* enter thou into the joy of thy lord" (Matthew 25:21).

It is a God-given principle that if we are faithful with the spiritual and material gifts that the Lord has blessed us with now, much more will be given to us in this life, as well as the life to come.

CHAPTER 23

GENTLENESS

Gentleness, which includes meekness and humility (Galatians 5:23, *The Amplified Bible*), is a much misunderstood gift of the Spirit. Many people subconsciously visualize a gentle or humble person as someone who is weak and spineless. Nothing could be further from the truth.

The Bible is full of teachings on humility and the dangers of the opposite which is pride. "God resisteth the proud, but giveth grace unto the humble" (James 4:6). The way of the cross is gentleness and humility.

Often we hide gentleness because we are afraid of being called soft or weak. We need to remind ourselves that gentleness is a divine trait.

The Lord Jesus said of Himself, "I am gentle and humble in heart" (Matthew 11:29 *NASB*). Yet there was an occasion when He took a whip and drove the money changers out of the Temple. Would you say that indicated weakness?

Moses is another great example of this gentleness. In Numbers 12:3 we read, "Now the man Moses was very humble, more than any man who was on the face of the earth" (*NASB*). Yet there was no one in the whole world of the Old Testament who exercised greater authority than he did.

Great men are invariably gentle men. In fact, only the truly humble are truly great. Nothing is so strong as gentleness, and nothing is so gentle as real strength.

Yet it is also true that great men *are* weak. Am I contradicting myself? No. The truth is that *all* men are weak. The only difference with the gentle man is that his eyes have been opened to this fact, and he has learned to lean upon the Lord.

Even the Son of God, co-equal with the Father in eternity, as man on earth, shared man's weakness. But because He was gentle or meek, Jesus drew His strength from the Father, enabling Him to move at all times in authority and power.

This principle which Jesus manifested in His own life on earth has to be worked out in our lives too if we would be like Him.

Obviously, a major point in a gentle person's life is his total realization of how much he depends upon the grace of God. He knows whenever he looks upon others less fortunate than himself that "There but for the grace of God go I."

He knows it is of the Lord's grace that he is able even to open his mouth and speak for Him. This is true whether it is on a one-to-one basis, preaching in a church, or speaking to a multitude in a mass crusade.

Yes, it is of the Lord's grace that we are able to speak for God. Unless we realize this, we get a superior attitude which is the exact opposite of gentleness or humility.

174

We in the Good News Crusade have just finished two tent crusades in Britain, and in thirty-five days counseled 1,200 persons. For England these days, that is quite something! Some of the miracles of healing were truly outstanding.

I remember as the crusades ended, I was so overwhelmed with the grace of God that I kept saying, first to the Lord, and then to other people, "I sure don't know why God uses us in this way." Certainly we don't deserve it. It is all of God's mercy.

The Christian man who is humble knows that without the Holy Spirit he would have absolutely nothing. No ability. No ministry. No gifts. No authority. No anything. In other words, gentleness is understanding that one is nothing but an earthen vessel, and all power and all blessing come from God alone.

It's good also to remind ourselves of the words of Paul—nearly his last words to a young man he loved very much in the faith. Paul desired that Timothy would rise even higher than himself and avoid some of the pitfalls of his own experience.

With this overwhelming feeling in his heart, he wrote to Timothy, "And the servant of the Lord must not strive; but be *gentle* unto all men" (2 Timothy 2:24). Then on another occasion he wrote to Titus, "Put them in mind... to speak evil of no man, to be no brawlers, but *gentle*, showing *all meekness* unto all men" (Titus 3:1,2). These were not easy words for Paul to write, but they were ones he wanted to express to these men of God, that they would show forth the fruit of gentleness.

James also wrote to young Christians, "But the wisdom that is from above is first pure, then peaceable, *gentle*, and easy to be entreated, full of mercy and good fruits, without partiality, and without hyprocrisy" (James 3:17).

Here we see that one of the ways to produce the fruit of the Spirit in our lives is to know the wisdom that comes from heaven, that comes from our all-wise Lord Who was so gentle, yet always so full of authority.

Another quality of gentleness is absolute trust and reliance upon this great wisdom of God.

When the Lord seems to keep us waiting for answers to our prayers, if we are gentle we will not go running ahead, forcing doors that He doesn't want opened. Even though others misunderstand and my look upon us as foolish, we remain meek and quiet, knowing that God is in control. We accept His rule in our lives rather than worrying about what others are saying.

It is good also to notice that in Psalm 25:9 God promises to guide the person who is meek; "The meek will he guide in judgement. . . ." Very often guidance goes wrong because of our own self-will, and our desire to please self rather than God. But it is easy for God to guide the person who is gentle or meek.

Have you ever seen a man taking his dog for a walk with the dog out in front dragging the man down the street? You look and wonder, "Now who is taking whom?"

But the well-disciplined dog, the one that respects his master's wishes, walks gently at his side with a loose lead. He can even be let off and trusted to heel. Wherever the man goes, the dog goes, because he has learned to be rightly related to his master. When we are rightly related to our Master, the Lord Jesus Christ, guidance becomes easy.

The same verse in Psalm 25 also says, ". . . the meek will he teach his way." The person who is gentle or meek is teachable. He knows there is always more to learn and has a desire to know the way of the Lord more perfectly.

Again in 1 Peter 3:3, 4, in the context of teaching wives to be subject to their own husbands, the writer describes gentleness as an ornament more beautiful than lovely clothes, gold trinkets, or smart hairdos (*NASB*).

As I write this, I am in the home of a person who travels around the world a good deal. On the mantlepiece in the lounge are three beautiful ornaments. They are so attractive that you can't help noticing them, and nearly everyone who comes into the home makes some comment about them.

Now, the kind of person referred to in Peter's epistle will be so attractive that you can't help noticing. But it won't be the things worn that catch your attention so much as the ornament of gentleness—the godlikeness of character.

Gentleness is also a quiet spirit. Some people who are not gentle are constantly agitating others. They cannot be around other people without disturbing them. But the people who are gentle are quiet and restful. They have learned to rest in the Lord, to relax in His presence. Consequently, they bring that restfulness into their relationships with other people.

Peter tells us that this ornament of a gentle and quiet spirit is of great price in the sight of God, and although in the immediate context this scripture is concerned specifically with wives, it is not to be thought that this only applies to them.

The whole passage from 1 Peter, 2:13 through to nearly the end of chapter three deals with the need to be subject to authorities and rulers and to be gracious to one another as brethren in the Lord.

It is evident then that the ornament of a gentle and quiet spirit is just as valuable to God displayed on a man as on a woman. We all need that beautiful ornament of gentleness and quietness and restfulness in God whether we are married, single, young, or old. For it is a precious fruit of the Spirit.

One Sunday school teacher shared a classroom situation concerning this fruit and the simple wisdom of a child. When she asked her class, "What is gentleness?" one little boy raised up his hand and said, "Gentleness is giving a soft answer to a rough question."

Another meaning of gentleness is "without feeling a spirit of revenge." I believe that to analyze this in yourself you need to be very honest, because a spirit of revenge can be a subtle thing.

It is something which I personally have to watch. It is quite a temptation to try to get back at someone in what I call a very "scientific" way. In other words, I have it all worked out in advance, even arranging the conversation just so. People might be thinking, "Oh, what a lovely person Don Double is," never realizing that I have manipulated things, because it all seems so sweet. But the spirit of revenge is there. This is a work of the flesh. The opposite of gentleness.

Gentleness always means not forcing your personality on other people, not pushing yourself forward, not always wanting to be in the picture, not pressing your point of view. Who is interested in your point of view? Or mine?

Gentleness sits back and speaks when spoken to, or when it has the Lord's point of view to give. If I have the word of the Lord for a situation, then of course I must give it. But if it is just my own opinion, it will not help much.

A gentle person is one who manifests the Lord Jesus Christ and lifts Him up, so that He is seen rather than self. The gentle man is a transparent man. There is nothing "put on"—no veneer.

One of the greatest testimonials one can give concerning another is "that person is so like the Lord. You can see Jesus in His face. When he speaks it is just like the Lord speaking to you."

John the Baptist said, "He must increase, but I must decrease" (John 3:30). The person who is gentle or humble has done away with the big "I" in his life. It would be worth taking stock one day and noticing how many times you say "I" or refer to yourself, especially when you are talking about the things of God. The gentle person is always pointing people to the Lord Jesus Christ. Gentleness is God-centered, never self-centered.

These are days when God is powerfully renewing His church. But it is often remarked that some people who have received the baptism in the Spirit tend to act and talk in a way that makes others feel like second-class Christians. That should not be.

A truly gentle ministry will make others hungry and thirsty for more of God, but it won't leave them feeling left out and pidgeonholed as second-class.

Gentleness is born out of a right relationship with God and will inevitably be manifested in our relationships with men. When we are manifesting gentleness, people will be aware not only of our presence, but also of the presence of God.

True gentleness has a lot to do with worship—with knowing God in reality. The word "worship" in the New Testament means "to kiss." To kiss you must be intimate. You cannot kiss a person from a distance.

One of the greatest verses in the Bible on worship is "Draw near to God and He will draw near to you"(James 4:8 *NASB*).

Therefore, when we are truly manifesting gentleness because of our relationship with God, people will not only be aware of us, but of Him too, because of His nearness to us.

You often hear people say, "I can't worship God because I don't feel like it. I don't feel like praising the Lord today." Doesn't that indicate that they have been worshiping their feelings rather than worshiping God? They feel good so they have a praise session. They don't feel in the mood so they don't praise God or worship Him.

We need to praise God because of Who He is; because we know Him in an intimate way; because we know His unchanging love, His ever increasing grace, His marvelous peace; because we know the beauty of His wonderful presence.

The man who worships, and who comes to know God in this intimate way, will be a gentle person and will carry the presence of God with him wherever he goes.

Such a person will be a man whose friendship is sought after and desired because he has answers for people's lives, and because he will bring them into the presence of the One Who can meet all their needs.

Cultivating the Fruit of Gentleness

Gentleness (or meekness) is a characteristic that is difficult for people to understand because of a fear that it will cause them to "lose their rights" or to be "walked on by others." But in Christ's example we can see that divine gentleness with the refusal to strike back, although it led Jesus to the cross, enabled Him to take His rightful and victorious seat at the right hand of the Father!

The Lord's gentleness
—Isaiah says of the Messiah, *"he ... shall gently lead* those that are with young" (Isaiah 40:11).

—David proclaims to the Lord, *"thy gentleness* hath made me great" (Psalm 18:35).

—Paul speaks of the *"gentleness of Christ"* (2 Corinthians 10:1).

—And James echoes "wisdom from above is ... *gentle"* (James 3:17).

—Finally, the Lord Jesus says of Himself, "for *I am gentle* and humble in heart" (Matthew 11:29 *NASB*).

Encouragement for gentleness
"Seek meekness" (Zephaniah 2:3) and *"put on a heart of...gentleness"* (Colossians 3:12 *NASB*) are words of wisdom for every Christian growing in the Spirit.

When Paul spoke of himself and those men that served with him, he stated, "But we were *gentle among you,* even as a nurse cherisheth her children" (1 Thessalonians 2:7). And then Paul encouraged anyone else who would desire to be a servant of Jesus, "the servant of the Lord must not strive; but *be gentle unto all men...In meekness* instructing those that oppose themselves" (2 Timothy 2:24,25).

Paul admonished the saints at Galatia and Ephesus to restore a brother who had sinned "in the *spirit of meekness"* (Galatians 6:1), and to "walk in a manner worthy of the calling with which you have been called, with all *humility and gentleness..."* (Ephesians 4:1,2 *NASB*).

Paul continues to speak about gentleness to Titus, encouraging him to remind all the brethren to be *"gentle,* showing *all meekness* unto all men" (Titus 3:2).

The rewards of gentleness and meekness
We have guidance: "The meek will he guide in

judgment: and the meek will he teach his way"
(Psalm 25:9).

We are uplifted: "The Lord lifteth up the meek"
(Psalm 147:6).

We are satisfied: "The meek shall eat and be
satisfied" (Psalm 22:26).

We have joy: "The meek also shall increase their
joy in the Lord" (Isaiah 29:19).

We have salvation: "For the Lord taketh pleasure
in his people: he will beautify the meek with
salvation" (Psalm 149:4); and the Bible says that
when God arises to judgment it will be "to save all
the meek of the earth" (Psalm 76:9).

We have a great inheritance: "Blessed are the
gentle, for they shall inherit the earth" (Matthew
5:5 *NASB*).

We have an inheritance and great peace: "But the
meek shall inherit the earth; and shall delight
themselves in the abundance of peace" (Psalm
37:11).

CHAPTER 24

SELF-CONTROL

The final fruit of the Spirit, self-control (temperance), is one of the most important keys to the Christian life.

By self-control we certainly do not mean legalism. Legalism produces a life that has no joy in it and brings a person under condemnation.

The Word of God is very clear in Romans 8:1 and 2. "There is *now* (note the time) no condemnation to them which are in Christ Jesus, who walk not after the flesh, but after the Spirit. For the law of the Spirit of life in Christ Jesus hath made me *free* from the law of sin and death."

Self-control, or temperance, is freedom not bondage, not a legalistic straight jacket. It is not following a book of do's and don'ts. Rather it is an expression of the deep life of Christ by the Holy Spirit that is within us.

Paul mentions more than once in his epistles that he regarded himself a prisoner of Jesus Christ. A love slave. Paul never admitted he was a prisoner of Rome, or of anyone else, but the prisoner of the Lord. It was a voluntary submission Paul made to the path Christ had chosen for him.

"We love him, because he first loved us" (1 John 4:19). This is where we find self-control. The free and happy man who is a prisoner of the Lord.

He is a living expression of the Creator's moral codes and, without a doubt, will shine in the fruit of self-control.

We see the opposite in those who throw away restraint and have no one to whom they submit or relate, who love and please only themselves. We see it in the drug scene, the alcoholic scene, the permissive society and broken homes. Through lack of self-control many destroy themselves, bringing grief and bondage into their lives, some even meeting with premature death.

There is no substitute for living the way God planned for us to live. He knows best. He knows what will bring us true joy and lasting happiness. Therefore, submitting to Him is the way to true freedom and abiding contentment.

Temptation is something that comes to every one of us, but temptation itself is not sin. It is only as we yield to temptation that we commit sin. Self-control is one of the answers to temptation.

A prominent psychiatrist has said that in nine out of ten cases where temptation is concerned, the ultimate disadvantages of sinning far outweigh the momentary satisfaction. He went on to show that drinking is only a temporary pleasure and not worth the hangover that results. The same goes for illicit encounters. The momentary satisfaction is like a drop in the ocean compared with the guilt and the other consequences that follow.

This same psychiatrist goes on to say that all of these things, in the end, produce guilt. As Christians, we can see that the fruit of self-control, our own self-life under the control of the Lord, prevents us from getting entangled in the destructive emotion of guilt.

A word that is hardly popular these days is the word "discipline." I remember the days when I had to do my National Service, and worked for her Majesty the Queen in the British Army. As I look back on those years when I was not a Christian and ran wild, I thank God that I learned a tremendous lot of discipline in the Army which has been invaluable when brought into my Christian life.

But the discipline of the Holy Spirit goes much deeper than that, and the first step towards knowing self under control of the Holy Spirit is a desire to live by the Word of God.

We need to realize that the Bible tells us the words Jesus Christ has spoken shall judge us in the last day (John 12:48). His words are spirit and life. Please note they are not spirit and legalism, but spirit and life. Nevertheless, they bring into our lives God's discipline.

Second Peter 1:6 NASB) says we are to add to knowledge, self-control. It is one thing to know God's Word, it is another thing to experience God's Word in every situation of life.

We need to recognize our weaknesses. Knowing our weaknesses can be Christ's strength to us. Knowing what God's Word says in a situation and turning our faith loose can bring self-control into manifestation and cause us to live in victory, when, otherwise, temptation would take us off into sin, and finally into guilt. For many Christians, the yielding to temptation and resulting guilt leads into a negative state that causes them to live for years in depression and frustration.

Weakness can be the greatest asset if, in a moment of temptation, we call upon Christ's strength and know self-control as a manifestation of the Holy Spirit in our lives.

The Bible tells us in Ephesians 5:18 to be filled with the Holy Spirit. This is prefaced by "And be not drunk with wine, wherein is excess. . . ." If we drink too much wine we become intoxicated and do all sorts of stupid things. But the parallel here is that by drinking of the Holy Spirit, and by yielding and submitting to the Holy Spirit, we can be filled with Him and under His control, manifesting the fruit of self-control and all the other fruit of the Spirit as well.

Through the indwelling Spirit, self can be under the control of the Lord, and we can live in victory—victory over temptation, victory over problems and difficulties, victory over sin.

The prodigal son left his father's house and threw self-control to one side, indulging in a wild life style. He ended up in the pigsty feeding the pigs. When he eventually came to himself, he went back to his father and said, "Father, I have sinned against heaven, and in your sight; I am no longer worthy to be called your son" (Luke 15:21 NASB). And immediately, in joy, his father forgave him, welcoming him back as a son.

If you have failed and gone away; if you have lived an intemperate life; if you have sinned in any way, there is forgiveness. There is the assurance of the Father's love if you come back and repent and rightly relate to the Lord again.

Finally, 1 Corinthians 9:25 says, "Everyone who competes in the games exercises self-control in all things" (*NASB*). For the Christian this will mean more than overcoming the grosser temptations of life. It will include exercising self-control in eating habits, sleeping habits, how much T.V. is watched, how long is spent staying up at night.

Self-control may also mean different things to different people depending on the manifestation of the self-life that is peculiar to their particular personality and background.

To live the kind of life that pleases God, we must submit totally to Jesus Christ. Only then will we know mastery over self that we need—and learn to have self-control in all things.

Cultivating the Fruit of Self-Control

In both the Old and New Testaments, believers are admonished to walk in self-control (or temperance) not allowing their human desires and impulses, or the flesh, to control them in any way. Here is some encouragement in cultivating the fruit of self-control in our lives.

The Bible often speaks of the Lord, Who is "slow to anger." This is a manner of self-control over our impulses and temper. The Bible says, *"He that is slow to anger is better than the mighty; and he that ruleth his spirit than he that taketh a city"* (Proverbs 13:32).

There are many words of caution given in the Scriptures concerning self-control. Solomon also warns, *"Like a city that is broken into and without walls is a man who has no control over his spirit"* (Proverbs 25:28 *NASB*). Paul cautions Timothy to *"flee youthful lusts"* (2 Timothy 2:22); and Peter echoes to all believers, *"Abstain from fleshly lusts..."* (1 Peter 2:11). While we flee these lusts and desires, we are to *"Let (our) moderation be known unto all men"* (Philippians 4:5).

In speaking to Titus, Paul states, *"The overseer must be* above reproach as God's steward

...sensible, just, devout, *self-controlled...*" (Titus 1:7,8 *NASB*). Paul also tells Titus to instruct all of the brethren *"to deny ungodliness and worldly desires* and to live sensibly, righteously and godly in the present age" (Titus 2:12 *NASB*).

The fruit of self-control is of such importance in the Christian life that Paul speaks very distinctly about the manifestation of it in his own life. He cries, "All things are lawful for me, but not all things are profitable. All things are lawful for me, *but I will not be mastered (enslaved) by anything"* (1 Corinthians 6:12 *NASB*).

Paul goes on to speak of the danger of not exercising self-control in all things as we walk in faith in Jesus Christ. He says to the church at Corinth, *"I buffet my body and make it my slave, lest possibly, after I have preached to others, I myself should be disqualified"* (1 Corinthians 9:27 *NASB*).

Finally, Paul speaks of our *reward for self-control;* we will receive a priceless gift which is imperishable—our eternal life. *"And everyone who competes in the games exercises self-control in all things. They then do it to receive a perishable wreath, but we an imperishable"* (1 Corinthians 9:25 *NASB*).

Let us therefore run the race God has set before us in self-control, *"in such a way that (we) may win!"* (1 Corinthians 9:24 *NASB*).

CHAPTER 25

THE NECESSITY OF FAITH

In closing, we must come to understand that all good things of the Spirit, whether the fruit or the gifts, come to us through the exercise of faith.

In counseling hundreds of people, I find one of the most common excuses people make for their failures is to imply that God has somehow let them down. "Well, I trusted the Lord," they will say, or "I did pray about it," as if God has been unfaithful in doing His part. Obviously, there was something lacking in their praying or "trusting."

The Bible makes it quite clear how we are supposed to trust the Lord, and this is the master key to every aspect of the Christian life. "Trust in the Lord with *all thine heart*" (Proverbs 3:5). Our trust must not be half-hearted, not just an intellectual exercise, but a child-like committal of faith.

This verse in Proverbs goes on to say, "Trust in the Lord with all thine heart; and *lean not unto thine own understanding*."

One of the reasons we lack faith is because we are

always trying to understand things with our minds. I must confess there are a lot of things I don't understand. But by the grace of God I am still willing to trust Him with all my heart.

Philemon 6 also tells us that the communication of our faith becomes effectual by the acknowledging of every good thing which is in us in Christ Jesus. Faith communicates all the good things that are in me in Christ, by the Holy Spirit.

My mind and my understanding will all the time be acknowledging the bad things that are in me of myself. But when I'm acknowledging with my heart the good things that are in me in Christ, then I am living the supernatural life of faith.

No matter what the failures of the past have been, we can make a new committal of our lives to Jesus, submitting our wills to Him, and trusting Him with all our hearts.

Then, as the Holy Spirit produces the gracious fruit of the Spirit in us, and manifests His gifts of power, it will be evident to all that we are living Life in a New Dimension.